BASS
RECORDED VERSIONS

BEST OF
BASS TAB

ISBN 978-1-4950-1073-6

HAL•LEONARD®
CORPORATION
7777 W. BLUEMOUND RD. P.O. BOX 13819 MILWAUKEE, WI 53213

Visit Hal Leonard Online at
www.halleonard.com

from Meghan Trainor - *All About That Bass*

All About That Bass

Words and Music by Kevin Kadish and Meghan Trainor

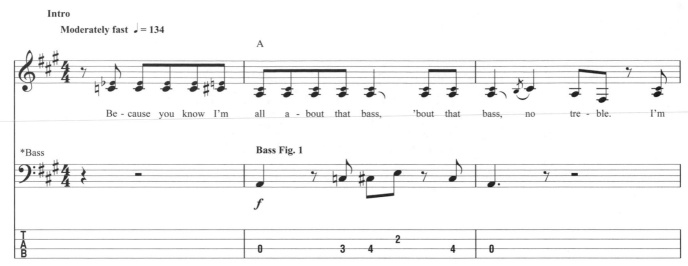

*Sampled upright bass arr. for elec. bass.

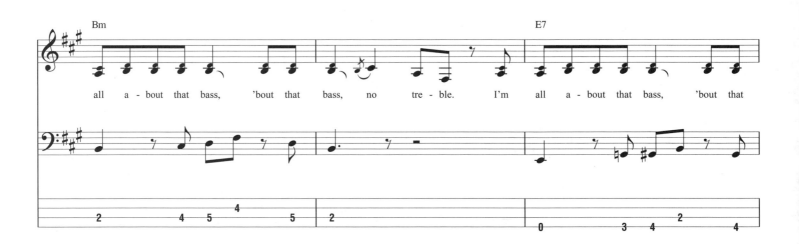

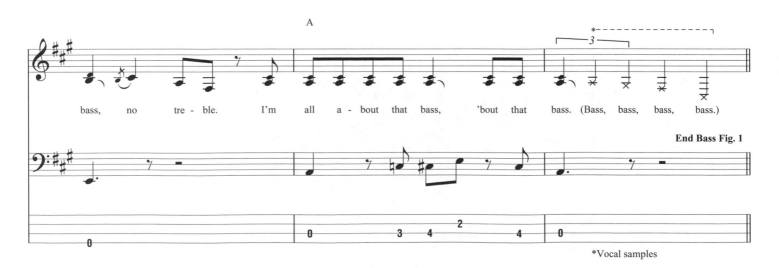

*Vocal samples

Verse

If you got beau-ty, beau-ty, just raise 'em up 'cause ev-'ry inch of you is per-fect from the bot-tom to the top. Yeah, my

Uh huh. Ev-'ry inch of you is per-fect from the bot-tom to the top.)

Pre-Chorus

ma-ma,__ she told me, "Don't wor-ry__ a-bout your size."__ She says,

Voc. Fig. 1

(Shoo wop, wop, sha-ooh wop, wop.

Bass Fig. 2

"Boys like __ a lit-tle __ more boo-ty __ to hold at night." __ You know I

That boo-ty, boo-ty. Uh, that boo-ty, boo-ty.

End Bass Fig. 2

4

Outro
Bass: w/ Bass Fig. 2 (1st 4 meas.)

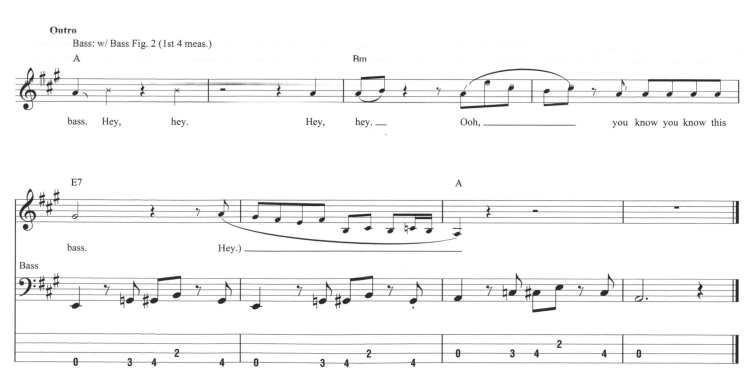

from Jet - *Get Born*

Are You Gonna Be My Girl

Words and Music by Cameron Muncey and Nicholas Cester

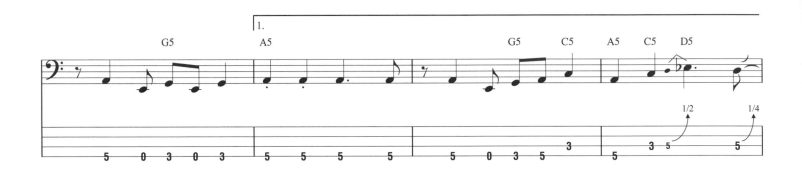

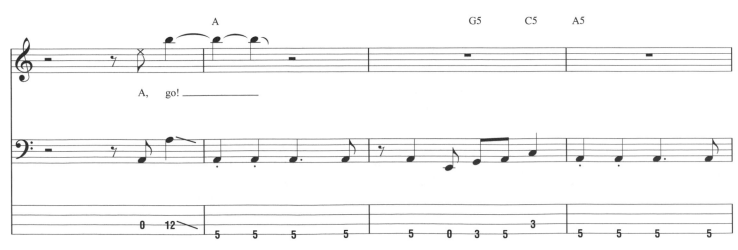

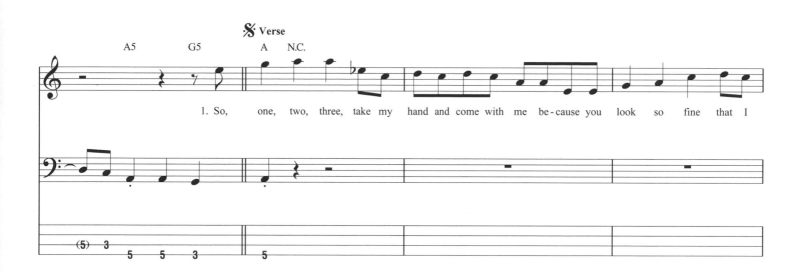

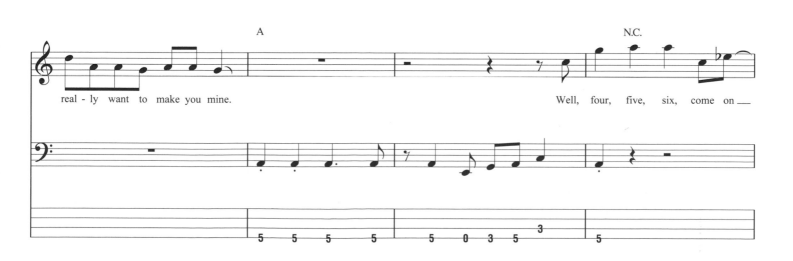

E5   F#5   G5

_____ and get your kicks. Now you don't need mon - ey { when you look like that, do you, hon - ey?
                                                        { with a face like that, do ya? _____

Bass: w/ Bass Fig. 1 (last 4 meas.)

A   C5   D5   A5   G5

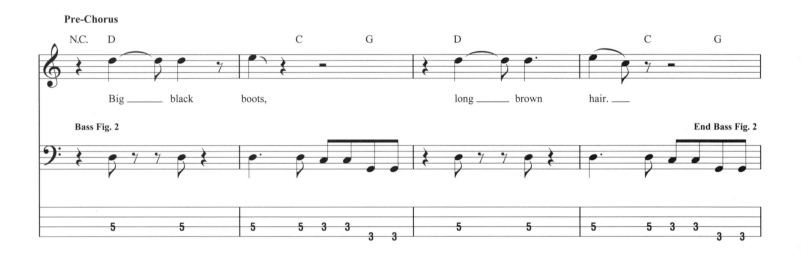

Pre-Chorus

N.C.   D   C   G   D   C   G

Big _____ black boots,   long _____ brown hair. _____

Bass Fig. 2   **End Bass Fig. 2**

5   5   5   5   3   3   5   5   5   5   3   3
                            3   3   3   3

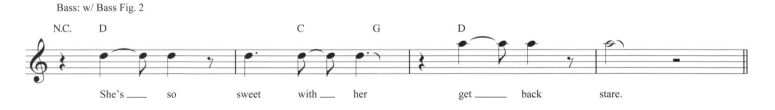

Bass: w/ Bass Fig. 2

N.C.   D   C   G   D

She's _____ so sweet with _____ her   get _____ back stare.

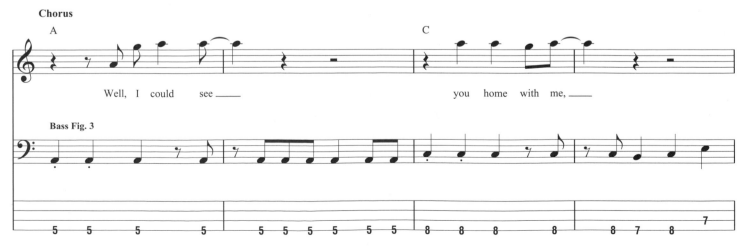

Chorus

A   C

Well, I could see _____   you home with me, _____

Bass Fig. 3

5   5   5   5   5   5   5   5   5   5   8   8   8   8   8   7   8   7

but you were with ___ an - oth - er man, ___ yeah. ___

End Bass Fig. 3

Bass: w/ Bass Fig. 3

I ___ know we ain't ___ got much to say ___

be - fore I let ___ you get a - way, ___ yeah. ___

To Coda ⊕

N.C. E   G   N.C.

I said, "Are you gon - na be

Interlude

Bass: w/ Bass Fig. 1

A

my girl?" ___

D.S. al Coda

C5 D5   A5   G5

2. Well, it's a

11

Coda

I said, "Are you gon-na be my girl?" —

Interlude

Ah,

Guitar Solo

yeah!

Ah,

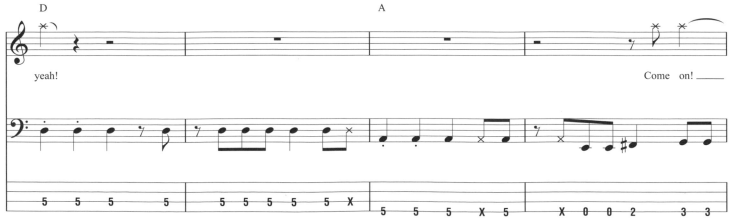

yeah!

Come on! _____

13

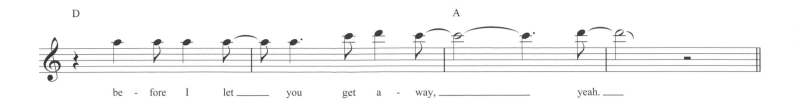

be - fore I let _____ you get a - way, _____ yeah. _____

Outro

Uh, be my girl. _____   Be _____ my   girl.

Are   you   gon - na   be _____ my   girl? _____

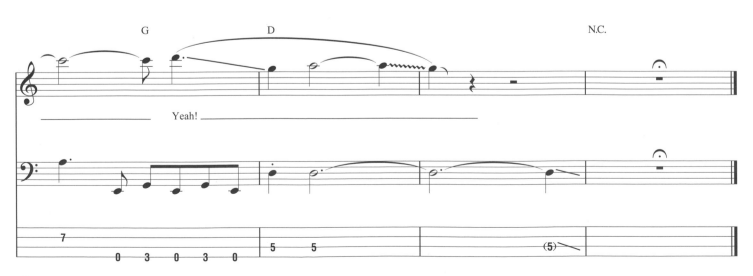

_____ Yeah! _____

14

from Red Hot Chili Peppers - *Californication*

Californication

Words and Music by Anthony Kiedis, Flea, John Frusciante and Chad Smith

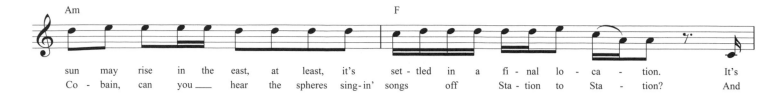

sun may rise in the east, at least, it's set-tled in a fi-nal lo-ca-tion. It's
Co-bain, can you hear the spheres sing-in' songs off Sta-tion to Sta-tion? And

To Coda ⊕

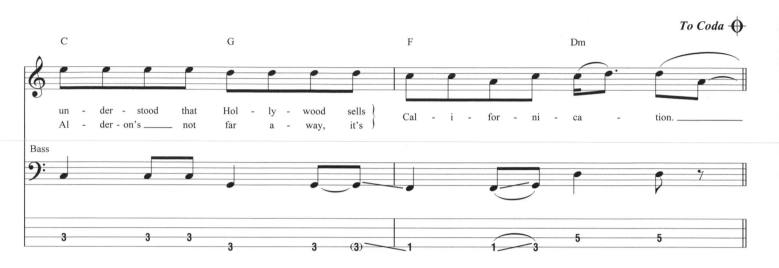

un-der-stood that Hol-ly-wood sells
Al-der-on's not far a-way, it's } Cal-i-for-ni-ca-tion.

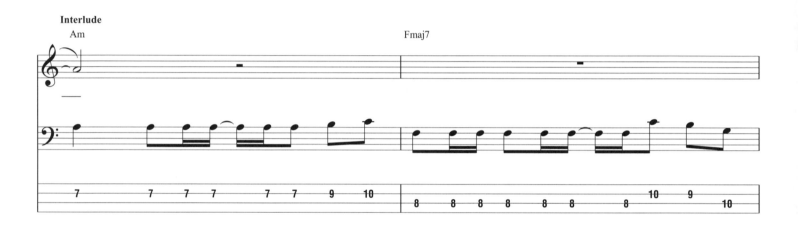

Interlude

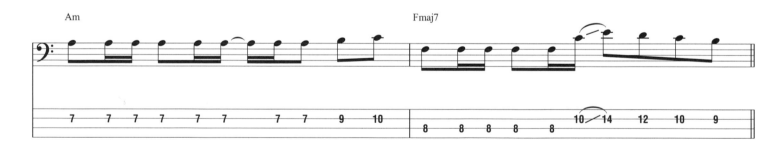

Pre-Chorus

Pay your sur-geon ver-y well to break the spell of ag-ing. Ce-

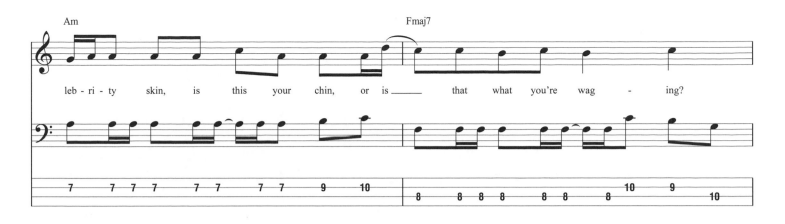

leb - ri - ty skin, is this your chin, or is _____ that what you're wag - ing?

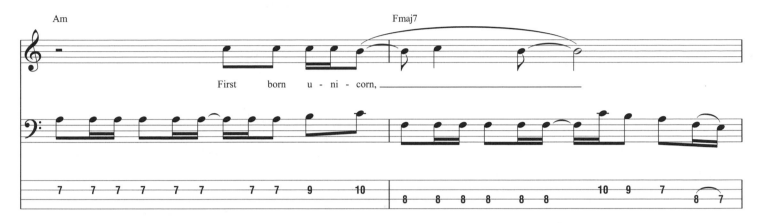

First born u - ni - corn, _____

hard - core _____ soft porn.

Chorus

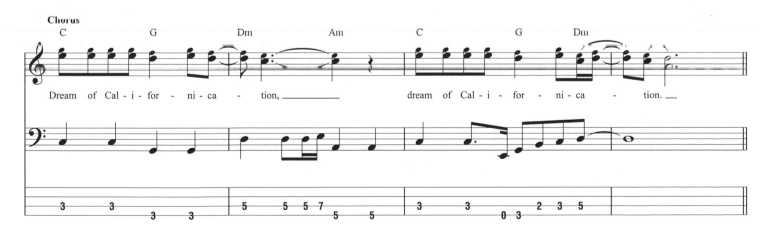

Dream of Cal - i - for - ni - ca - tion, _____ dream of Cal - i - for - ni - ca - tion. _____

D.S. al Coda

Interlude
Bass: w/ Bass Fig. 1

Am   F   Am   F

⊕ Coda

Interlude

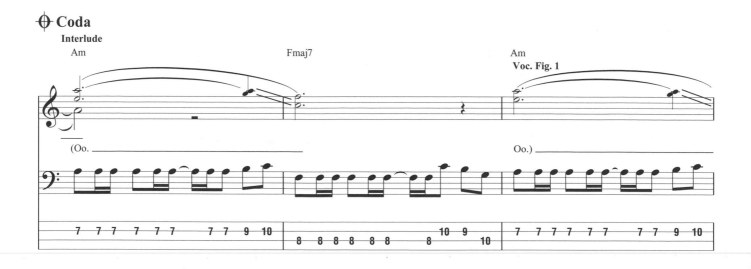

(Oo. _____ Oo.) _____

Pre-Chorus

Bkgd. Voc.: w/ Voc. Fig. 1 (4 times)

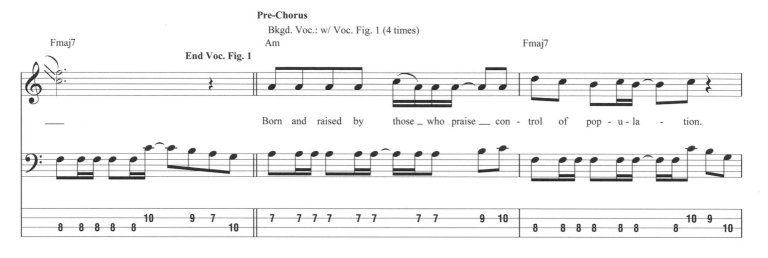

___ Born and raised by those __ who praise __ con - trol of pop - u - la - tion.

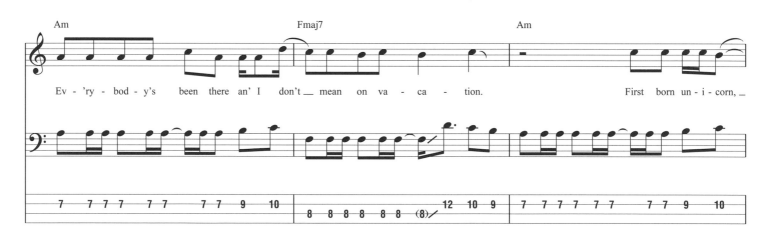

Ev - 'ry - bod - y's been there an' I don't __ mean on va - ca - tion. First born un - i - corn, __

hard - core _____ soft porn.

18

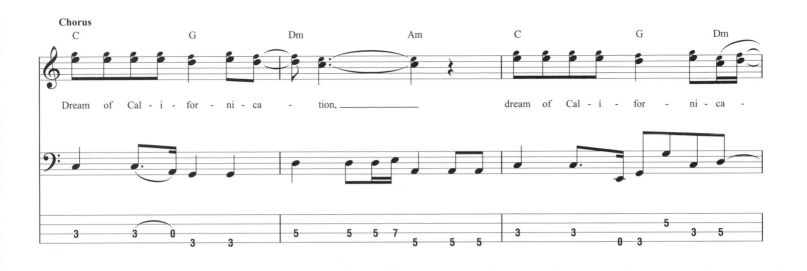

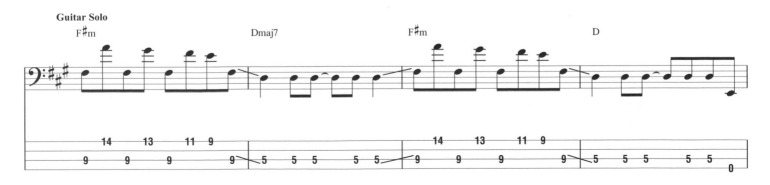

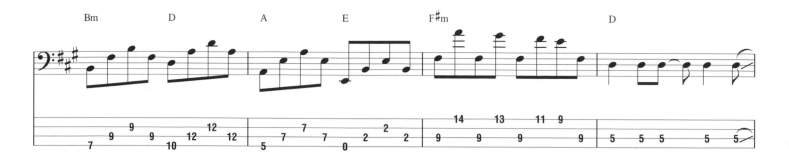

Interlude
Bass: w/ Bass Fig. 1

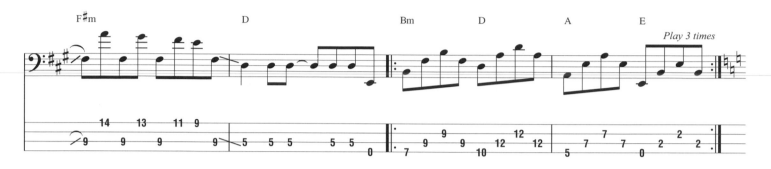

5. De -

Verse
Bass: w/ Bass Fig. 1

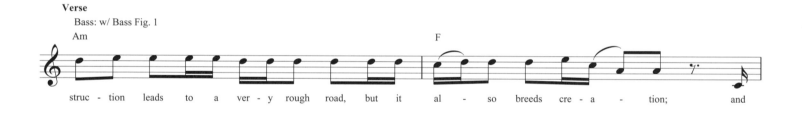

struc - tion leads to a ver - y rough road, but it al - so breeds cre - a - tion; and

earth - quakes are to a girl's gui - tar, they're just an - oth - er good vi - bra - tion. And

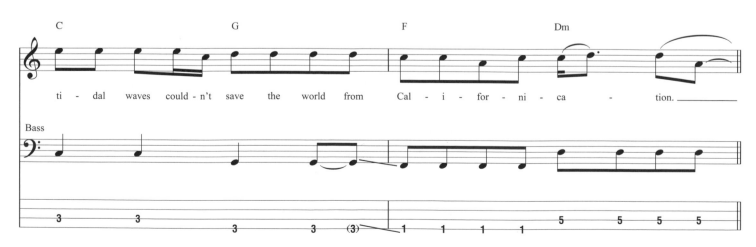

ti - dal waves could - n't save the world from Cal - i - for - ni - ca - tion.

Interlude

Bkgd. Voc.: w/ Voc. Fig. 1 (2 times)

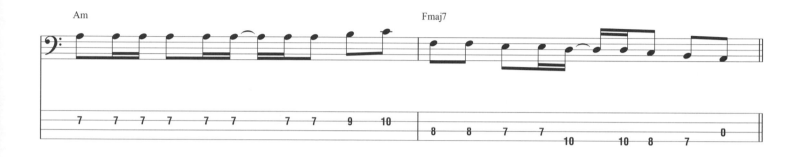

Pre-Chorus

Bkgd. Voc.: w/ Voc. Fig. 1 (4 times)

Pay your sur - geon ver - y well to break __ the spell of ag - ing.

Sick - er than the rest, there is __ no test, but this __ is what you're crav - ing. __

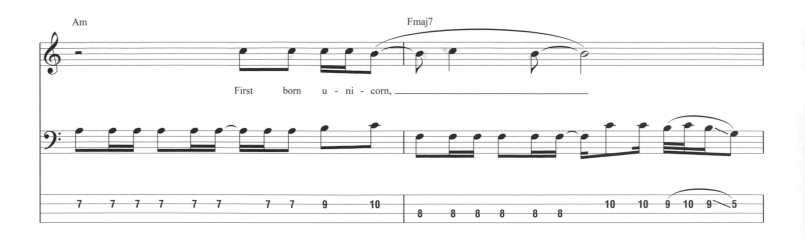

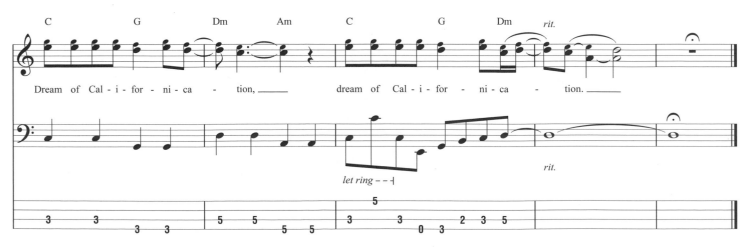

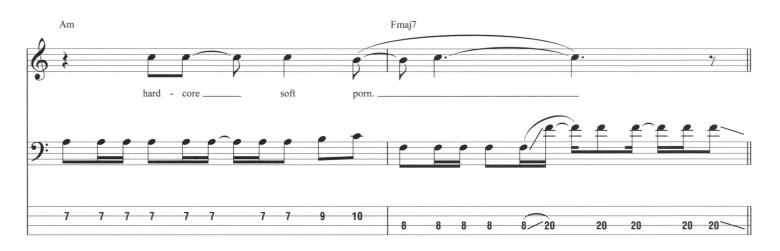

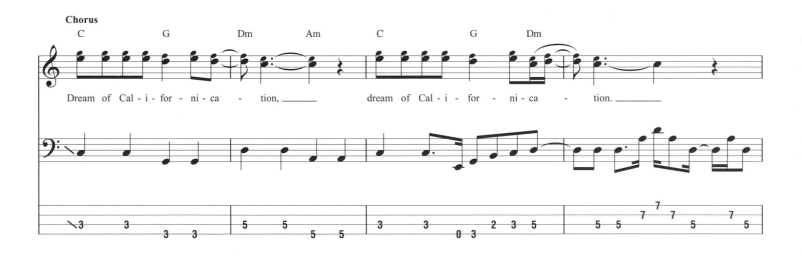

Do I Wanna Know?

Words by Alex Turner
Music by Arctic Monkeys

(D5) (G5)

spil - lin' ___ drinks ___ on ___ my ___ set - tee. (Do I wan -

Bass Bass Fill 1 End Bass Fill 1

% **Pre-Chorus**

(E♭) (C5) (G5)

- na know) ___ if this feel - ing flows ___ both ways? ___ (Sad to see ___ you go;) ___ was sort of hop-

Bass Fig. 2 End Bass Fig. 2

2nd time, Bass: w/ Bass Fig. 2

(E♭) (C5)

- ing that ___ you'd stay. (Ba - by, we ___ both know) ___ that the nights ___ were main - ly made ___ for say - ing things ___

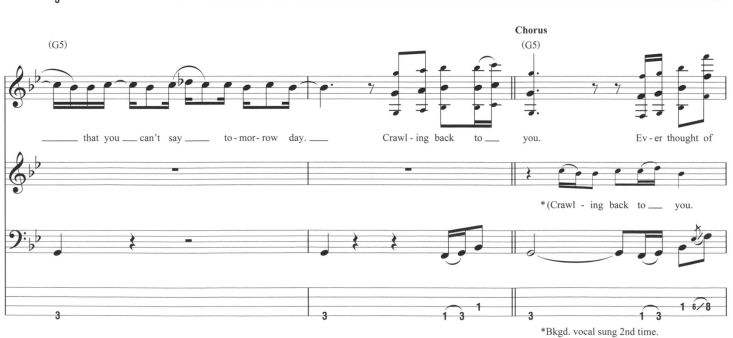

(G5) **Chorus** (G5)

___ that you ___ can't say ___ to - mor - row day. ___ Crawl - ing back to ___ you. Ev - er thought of

*(Crawl - ing back to ___ you.

*Bkgd. vocal sung 2nd time.

Everlong

Words and Music by David Grohl

Drop D tuning:
(low to high) D-A-D-G

Intro

Moderately fast ♩ = 158

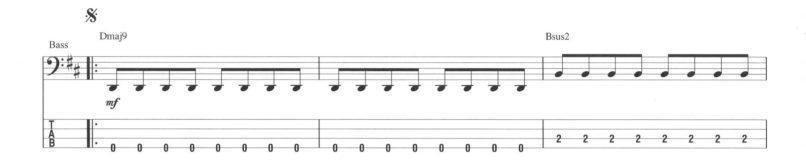

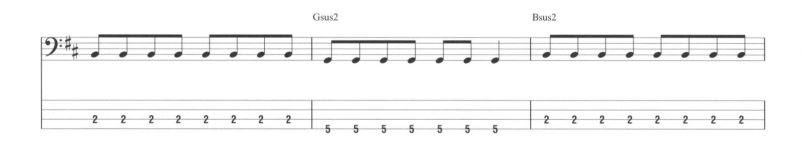

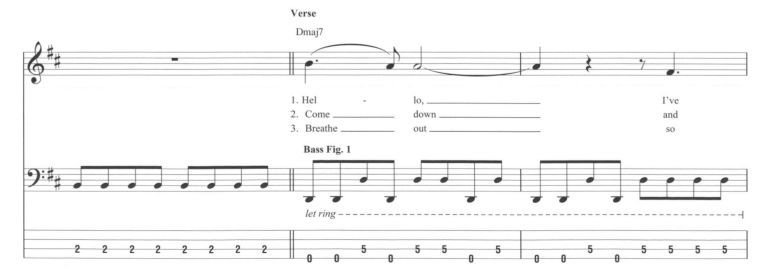

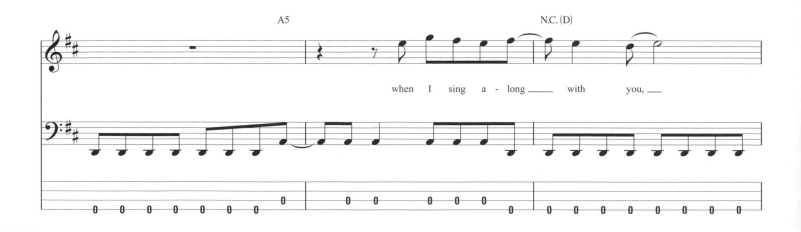

when I sing a - long ___ with you, ___

§.§ Chorus

if ev - 'ry - thing could ev - er feel this real ___ for - ev -

*Sing vocal harmony 2nd & 3rd times only.

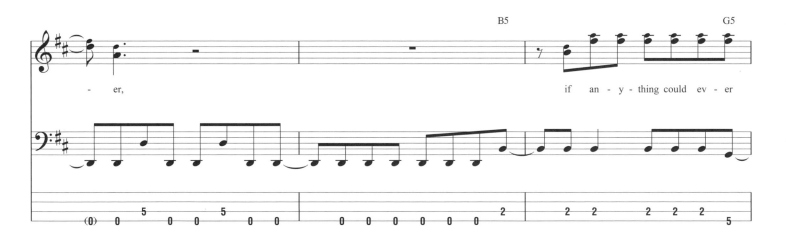

- er, if an - y - thing could ev - er

be this good ___ { 1. a - gain.
{ 2., 3. a - gain. ___ }

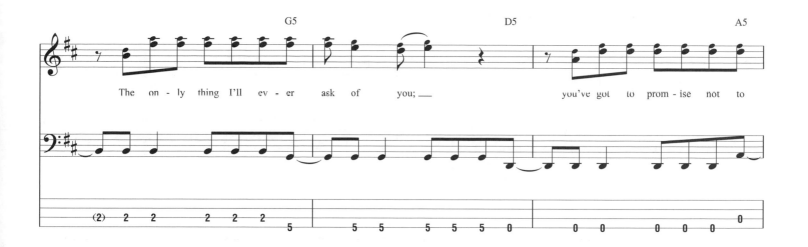

The on-ly thing I'll ev-er ask of you;___ you've got to prom-ise not to

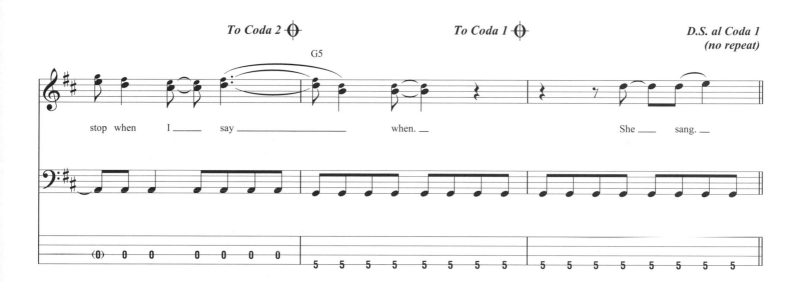

To Coda 2 ⊕ *To Coda 1* ⊕ *D.S. al Coda 1*
(no repeat)

stop when I ___ say _____ when. ___ She ___ sang. ___

⊕ **Coda 1**

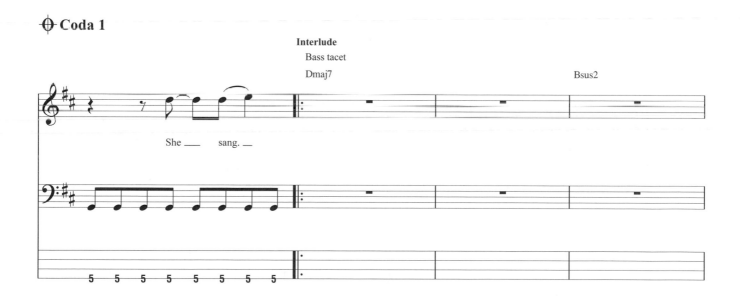

Interlude
Bass tacet
Dmaj7 Bsus2

She ___ sang. ___

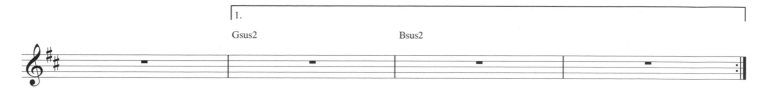

1.
Gsus2 Bsus2

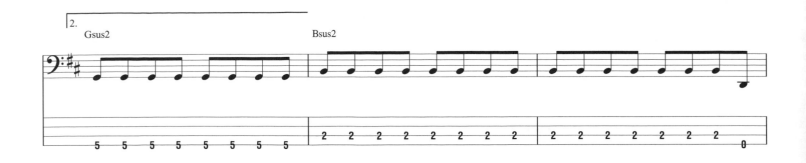

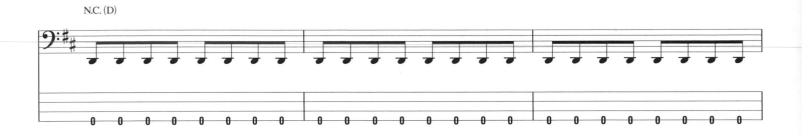

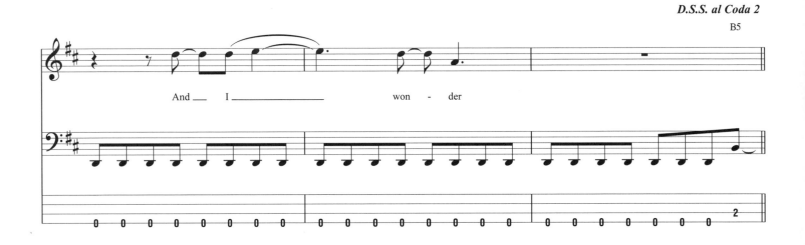

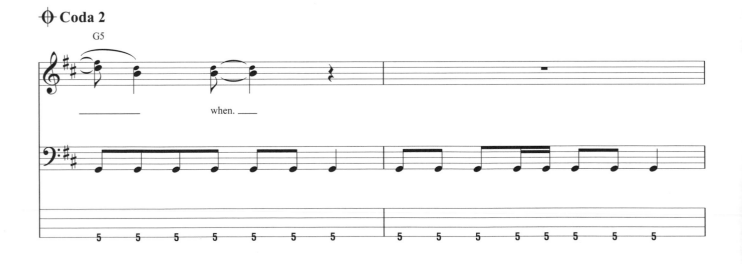

from Gorillaz - *Demon Days*

Feel Good Inc

Words and Music by Damon Albarn, Jamie Hewlett, Brian Burton and De La Soul

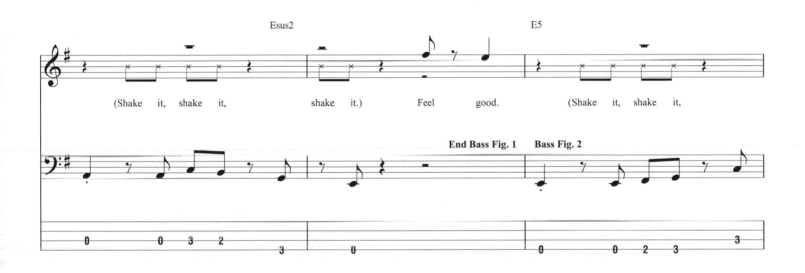

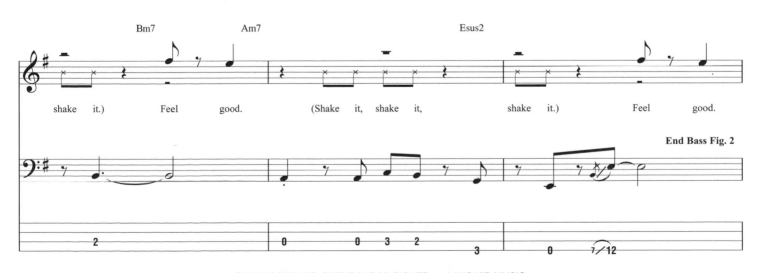

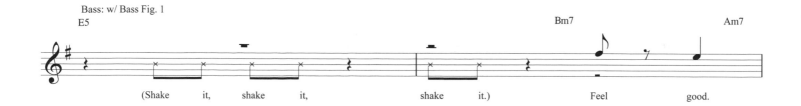

(Shake it, shake it, shake it.) Feel good.

Verse
Bass: w/ Bass Fig. 2 (4 times)

(Shake it, shake it, shake it.) Feel good. 1. Ci - ty's break - ing down on a

cam - el's back, they just have to go 'cause they don't know whack. So

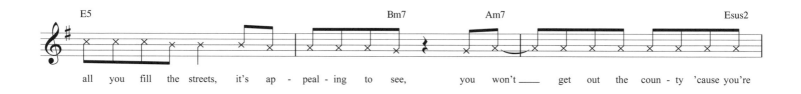

all you fill the streets, it's ap - peal - ing to see, you won't _____ get out the coun - ty 'cause you're

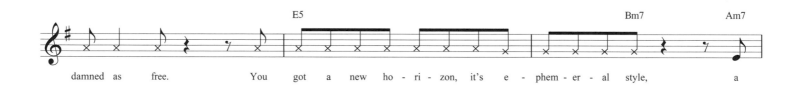

damned as free. You got a new ho - ri - zon, it's e - phem - er - al style, a

mel - an - cho - ly town where we nev - er smile. ___ And all I wan - na hear is the

mes - sage beep; my dreams, ___ they've got - ta kiss be - cause I don't get sleep, ___ no.

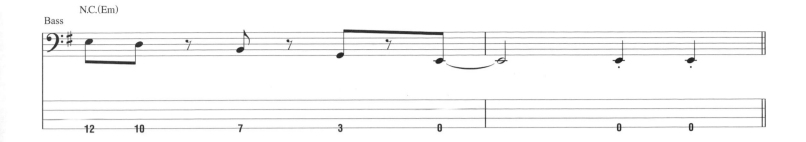

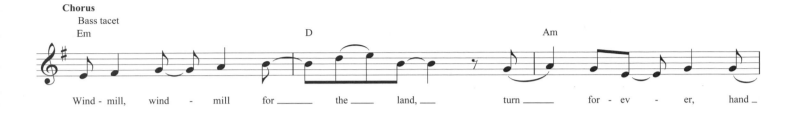

Chorus
Bass tacet

Wind - mill, wind - mill for _____ the _____ land, _____ turn _____ for - ev - er, hand _____

_____ in _____ hand. Take it all _____ in on _____ your stride, _____

it is tick - ing fall _____ ing down. Love for - ev - er, love _____

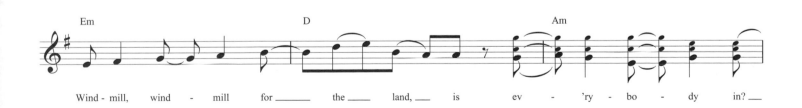

to free, _____ lets turn _____ for - ev - er, you _____ and _____ me.

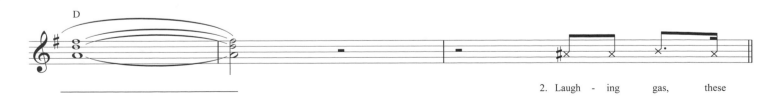

Wind - mill, wind - mill for _____ the _____ land, _____ is ev - 'ry - bo - dy in? _____

_____ 2. Laugh - ing gas, these

Verse

Bass: w/ Bass Fig. 1

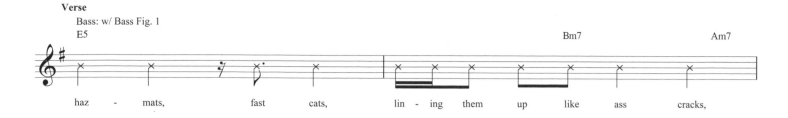

haz - mats, fast cats, lin - ing them up like ass cracks,

la - dies, po - nies at the track, it's my choc - o - late at - tack. _____

Bass: w/ Bass Fig. 2

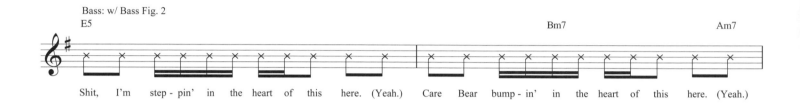

Shit, I'm step - pin' in the heart of this here. (Yeah.) Care Bear bump - in' in the heart of this here. (Yeah.)

Watch me as I grav - i - tate, ha - ha - ha - ha - ha - ha. _____ Yo, we go - in'

Bass: w/ Bass Fig. 1

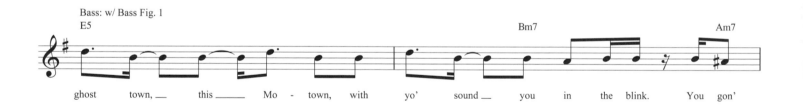

ghost town, __ this _____ Mo - town, with yo' sound __ you in the blink. You gon'

bite the dust, __ can't fight with us, _____ with yo' sound __ you kill the Inc. So

Bass: w/ Bass Fig. 2 (1 1/2 times)

don't stop, get it, get it, un - til you jet a - head. Yo, watch the way I nav - i - gate, ha -

ha - ha - ha - ha. _____   (Shake it, shake it,   shake it.)   Feel   good.

Breakdown

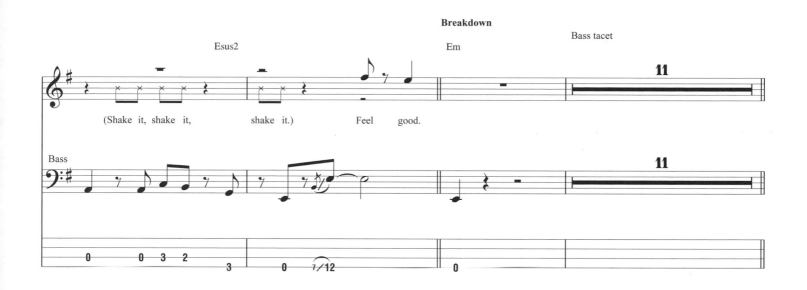

(Shake it, shake it,   shake it.)   Feel   good.

Chorus

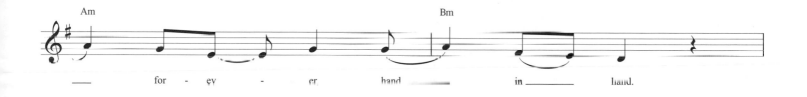

Wind - mill,   wind - mill   for _____   the _____   land, _____   turn _____

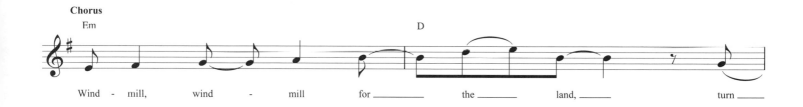

_____   for - ev - er   hand _____   in _____   hand.

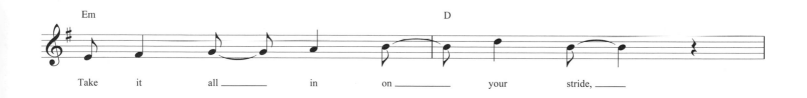

Take   it   all _____   in   on _____   your   stride, _____

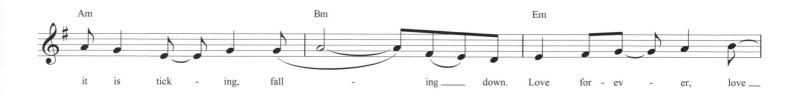

it   is   tick - ing,   fall - ing _____   down.   Love   for - ev - er,   love _____

_____ is free, _____ let's turn _____ for - ev - er, _____ you _____ and _____ me.

Wind - mill, wind - mill for _____ the _____ land, _____ is ev - 'ry - bod - y in? _____

Verse
Voc.: w/ Voc. Fig. 1 (4 times)
1st time, Bass: w/ Bass Fig. 2
2nd time, Bass: w/ Bass Fig. 1

3. Don't _____ stop, _____ get it, get it, we are your cap - tains in it.

Stead - y, watch me nav - i - gate, ha - ha - ha - ha - ha - ha. _____

Outro
1st time, Bass: w/ Bass Fig. 2
2nd time, Bass: w/ Bass Fig. 1

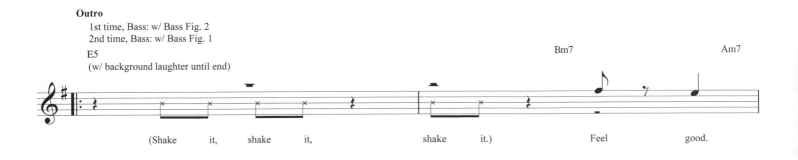

(w/ background laughter until end)

(Shake it, shake it, shake it.) Feel good.

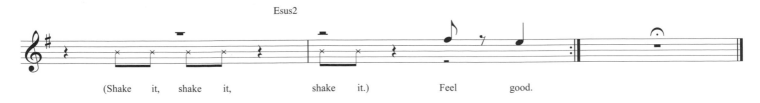

(Shake it, shake it, shake it.) Feel good.

from Daft Punk - *Random Access Memories*

Get Lucky

Words and Music by Thomas Bangalter, Guy Manuel Homem Christo, Pharrell Williams and Nile Rodgers

we're up ___ all night ___ to get ___ luck - y. We're up ___ all night ___ to get ___ luck - y. We're up ___ all night ___ to get ___ luck - y.

We're up ___ all night ___ to get ___ luck - y. We're up ___ all night ___ to get ___ luck - y.

Bass tacet
Bm   D   F#m   E   **End Voc. Fig. 1**

Voc. Fig. 1

*(We're up   all night   to get,   we're up   all night   to get,   we're up   all night   to get,   we're up   all night   to get.)

*Processed w/ vocoder

Bkgd. Voc.: w/ Voc. Fig. 1
Bm   D

**(We're up   all night   to   get,   to - geth -   er,   all   night   to   get   to - geth -

**As before

Voc. Fig. 2

(We're up all night __ to get luck - y. We're up all night __ to get luck - y.

End Voc. Fig. 2

We're up all night __ to get luck - y. We're up all night __ to get luck - y.)

Pre-Chorus

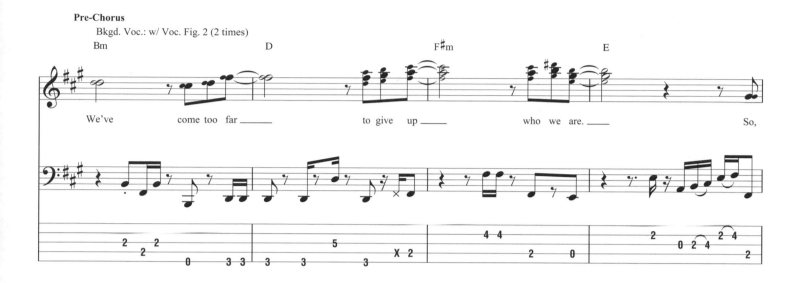

We've come too far _____ to give up _____ who we are. _____ So,

let's raise the bar _____ and our cups _____ to the stars. _____

Chorus

She's up _____ all night _____ till the sun, I'm up _____ all night _____ to get some.

Bass Fig. 1

She's up ___ all night ___ for good fun,   I'm up ___ all night ___ to get luck - y.

End Bass Fig. 1

Bass: w/ Bass Fig. 1 (2 1/2 times)

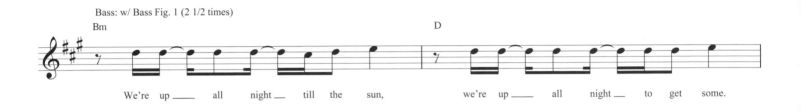

We're up ___ all night ___ till the sun,   we're up ___ all night ___ to get some.

We're up ___ all night ___ for good fun,   we're up ___ all night ___ to get ___ luck - y.

We're up ___ all night ___ to get ___ luck - y.   We're up ___ all night ___ to get ___ luck - y.

We're up ___ all night ___ to get ___ luck - y.   We're up ___ all night ___ to get ___ luck - y.

We're up ___ all night ___ to get ___ luck - y.   We're up ___ all night ___ to get ___ luck - y.

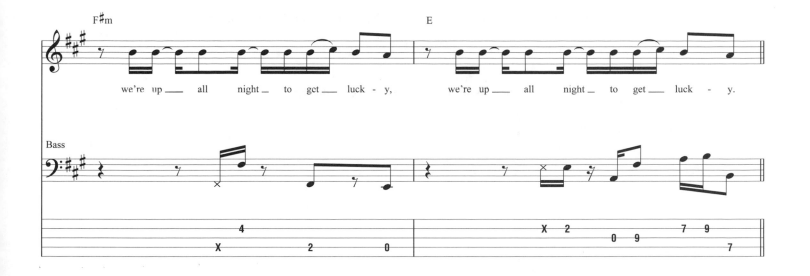

we're up ___ all night ___ to get ___ luck - y,   we're up ___ all night ___ to get ___ luck - y.

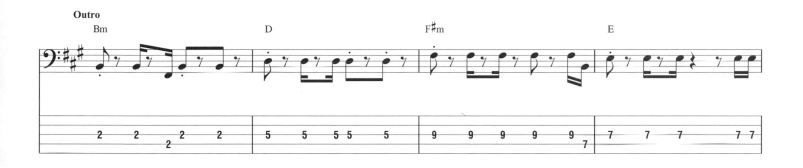

Outro

Begin fade

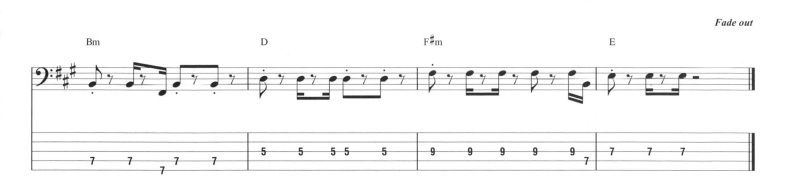

Fade out

from Pharrell Williams - *Despicable Me 2 (Original Motion Picture Soundtrack)*

Happy

from DESPICABLE ME 2
Words and Music by Pharrell Williams

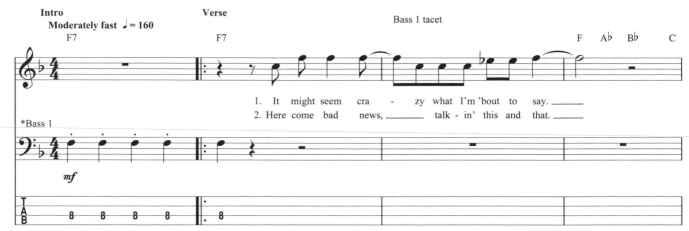

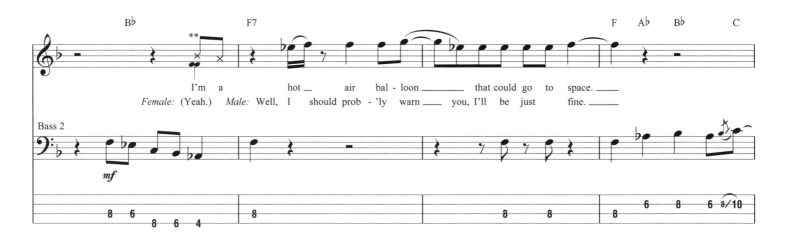

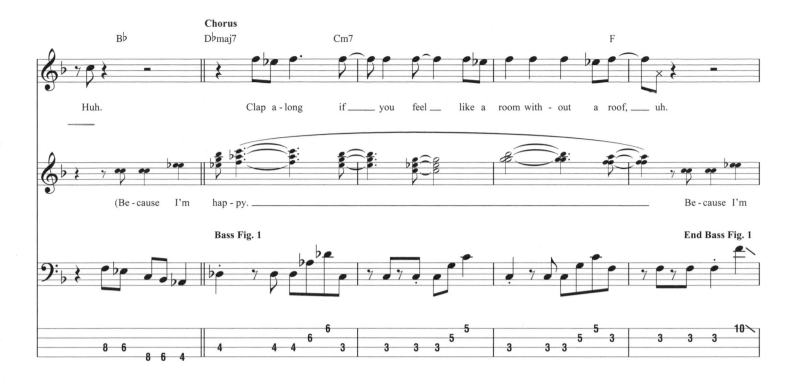

from Muse - *Absolution*

Hysteria

Words by Matthew Bellamy
Music by Matthew Bellamy, Chris Wolstenholme and Dominic Howard

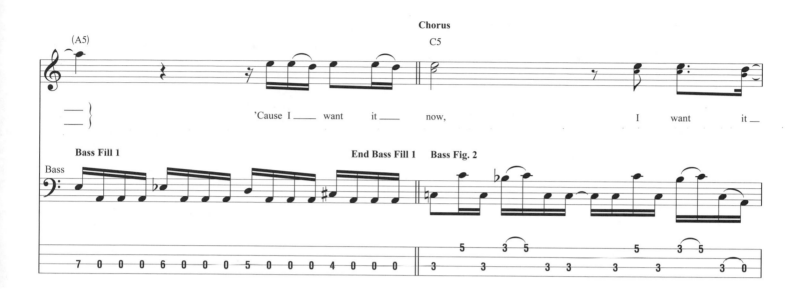

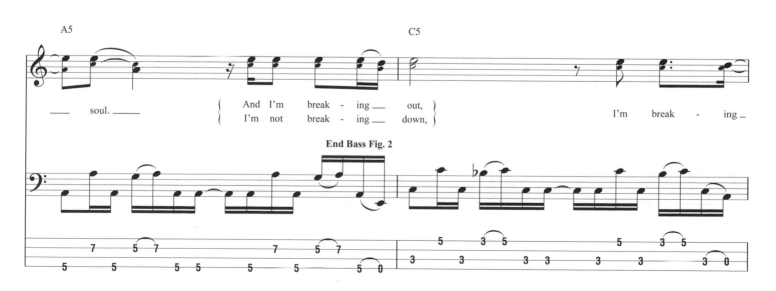

out. _____

A - last chance to lose con - trol. ____

Interlude

Bass: w/ Bass Fig. 1

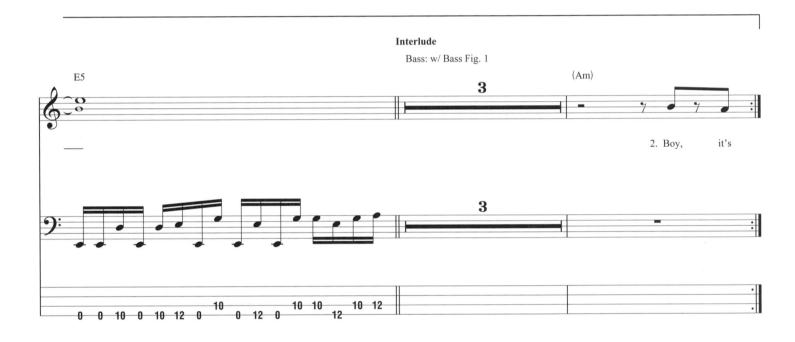

(Am)

2. Boy, it's

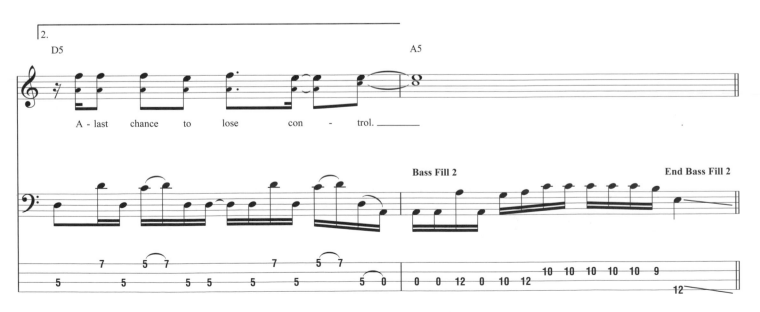

A - last chance to lose con - trol. _____

Bass Fill 2

End Bass Fill 2

Interlude

N.C.(E5)

Guitar Solo

Bass: w/ Bass Fig. 1 (1 3/4 times)   Bass: w/ Bass Fill 1   Bass: w/ Bass Fig. 2 (2 times)

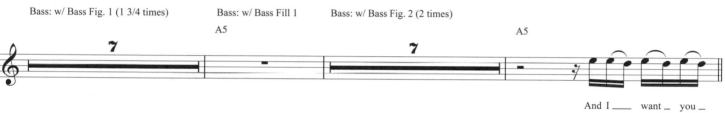

And I ___ want _ you _

Chorus

Bass: w/ Bass Fig. 2 (1 3/4 times)

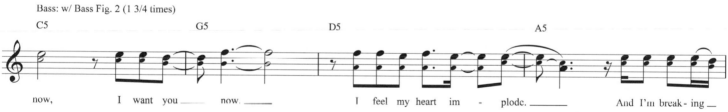

now,   I want you ___ now. ___   I feel my heart im - plode. ___   And I'm break-ing _

Bass: w/ Bass Fill 2

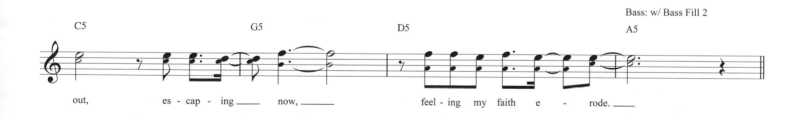

out,   es - cap - ing ___ now, ___   feel-ing my faith e - rode. ___

Outro

N.C.(E5)

Play 5 times

Bass

from Pearl Jam - *Ten*

Jeremy

Music by Jeff Ament
Lyric by Eddie Vedder

Intro
Moderately slow ♩ = 96

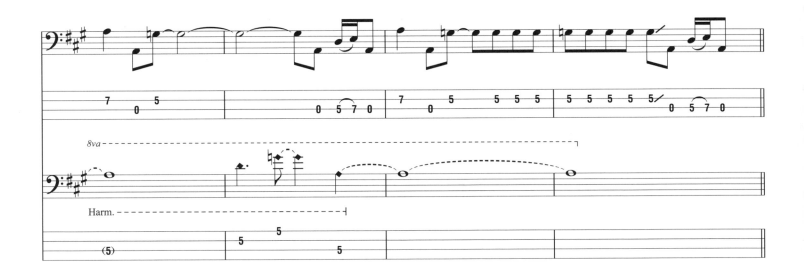

* Each string (E A D G) is tripled, with a second string 8va, and a third string 15ma.

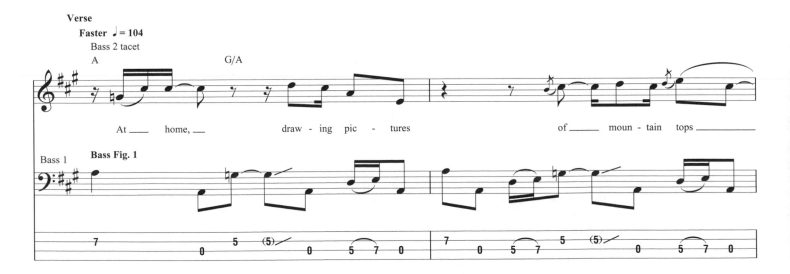

with ___ him on ___ top, lem - on yel - low - sun, ___

End Bass Fig. 1

Bass 1: w/ Bass Fig. 1

___ arms ___ raised ___ in a V, and the dead lay ___ in pools of ma - roon be - low.

Dad - dy did - n't give at - ten - tion, ___

Bass Fig. 2

Bass 1

*Chords refer to guitar.

oh, ___ to the fact that Mom - my ___ did - n't care. ___ King ___

___ Jer - e - my ___ the wick - ed, ___ oh, ___ ruled his world. ___

End Bass Fig. 2

57

Chorus

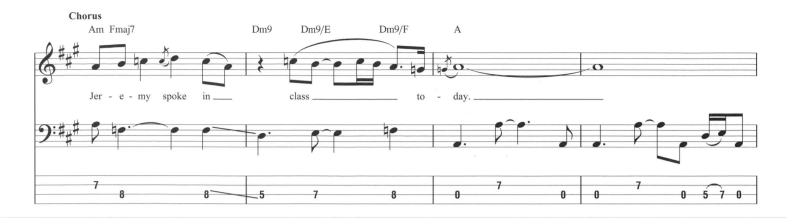

Jer - e - my spoke in class to - day.

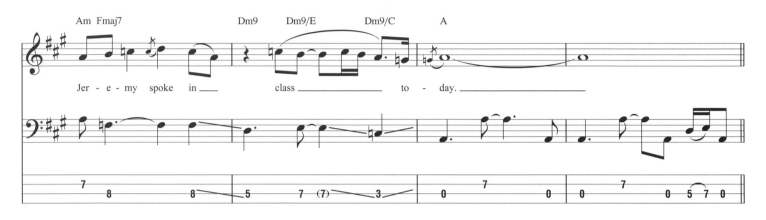

Jer - e - my spoke in class to - day.

Verse

Bass: w/Bass Fig. 1 (4 times)

Clear - ly I re - mem - ber pick - ing on the boy,

seemed a harm - less lit - tle fuck.

Oo, but we un - leashed a li - on. Gnashed

his teeth and bit the re - cess lad - y's breast, how could I for -

get? And he hit me with a sur - prise left. My jaw left hurt - in',

oo, _____ dropped wide o - pen   just like _____ the day, _____

Bass 1: w/ Bass Fig. 2

_____   oh, _ like the _ day I heard. _____   Dad - dy did - n't

give af - fec - tion,   no, _____   and the boy   was   some - thing   that Mom - my would - n't

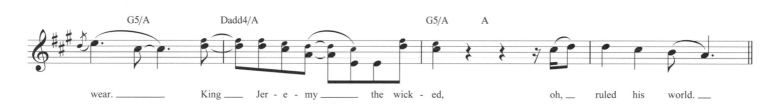

wear. _____   King _ Jer - e - my _____ the wick - ed,   oh, _ ruled his world. _

Chorus

Jer - e - my spoke in _____   class _____ to - day. _____
                                              (day.) _____

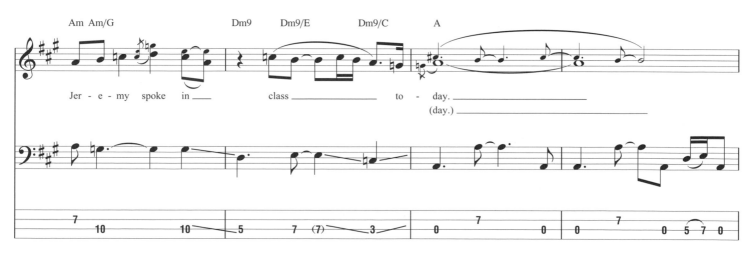

Jer - e - my spoke in _____   class _____ to - day. _____
                                              (day.) _____

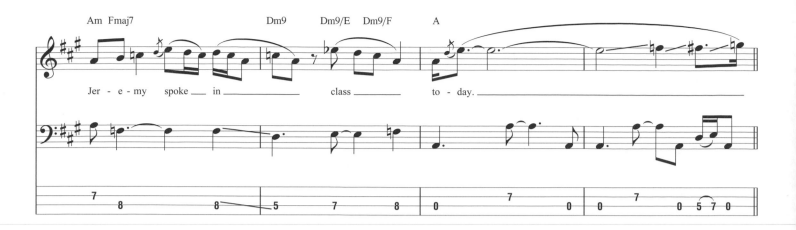

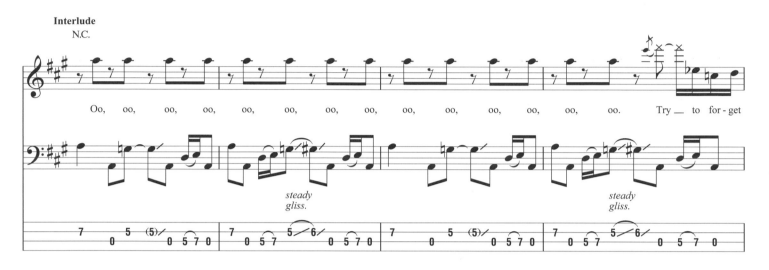

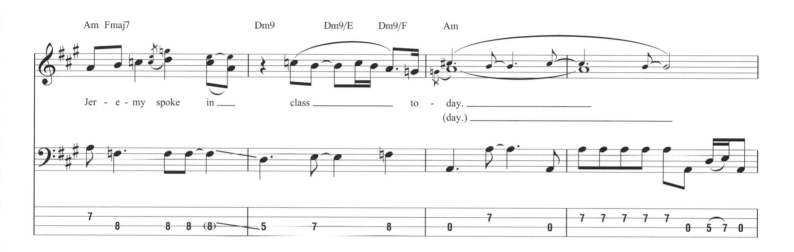

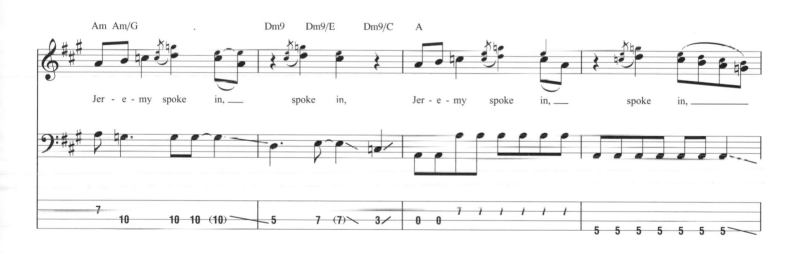

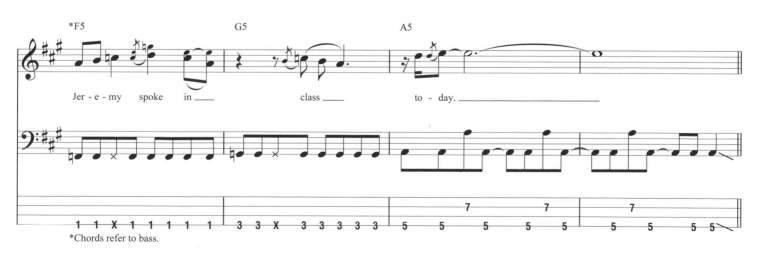

*Chords refer to bass.

Outro

w/ Vocal ad lib.

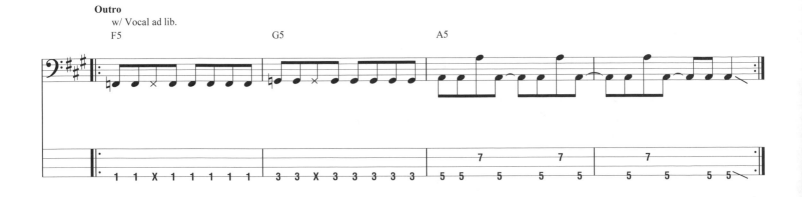

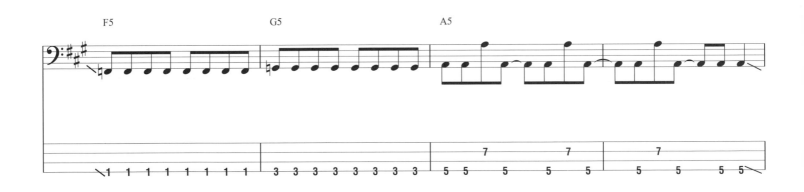

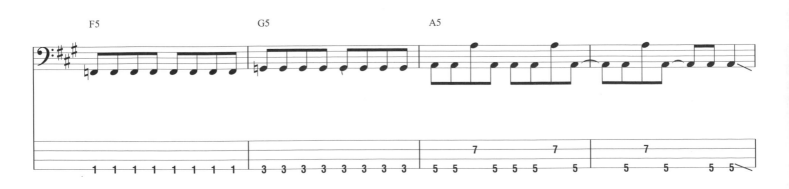

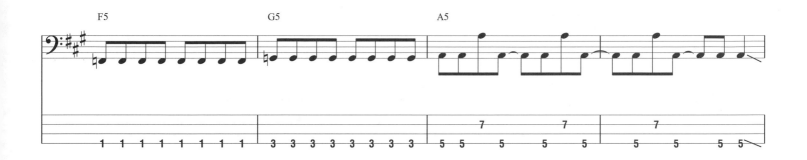

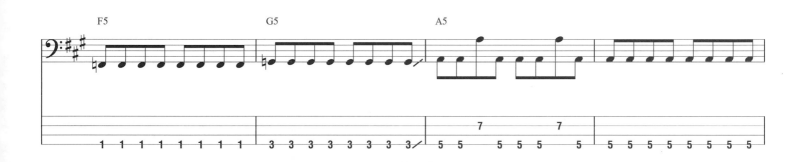

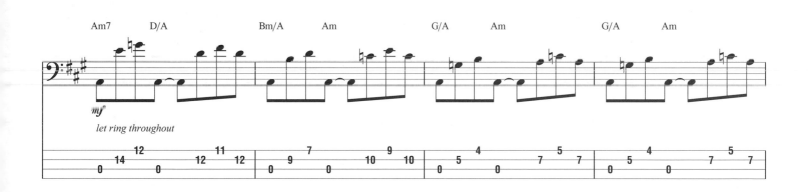

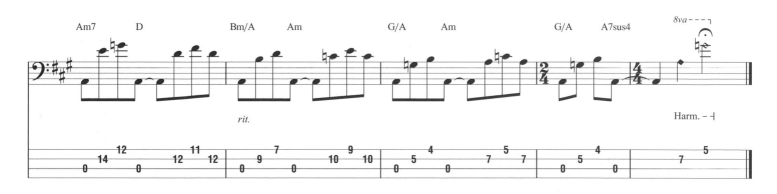

Let's Get It Started

Words and Music by Will Adams, Allan Pineda, Jaime Gomez, Michael Fratantuno, George Pajon Jr. and Terence Yoshiaki

*Gang vocals

Pre-Chorus

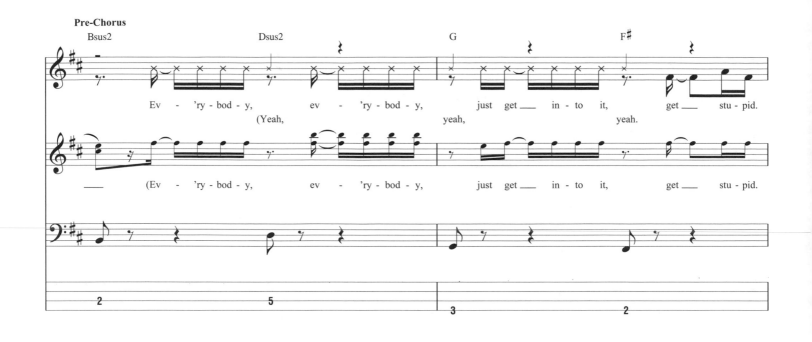

Ev - 'ry-bod - y,   ev - 'ry-bod - y,   just get ___ in - to it,   get ___ stu - pid.

(Ev - 'ry-bod - y,   ev - 'ry-bod - y,   just get ___ in - to it,   get ___ stu - pid.

Get it start - ed,   get it start - ed,   get it start - ed.   Let's get it

Come on,   come on,   yeah!)

Get it start - ed,   get it start - ed,   get it start - ed.)

Chorus

Bass: w/ Bass Fig. 1 (2 times)

start - ed, ___ ha!   Let's get it   start - ed in here. ___ Let's get it   start - ed, ___ ha!   Let's get it

start - ed in here. ___ Let's get it   start - ed, ___ ha!   Let's get it   start - ed in here. ___ Let's get it

Voc. Fig. 1   **End Voc. Fig. 1**

(Ha, ha, ha, ha, ha, ha, ha,   ha, ha, ha, ha, ha, ha, ha.)

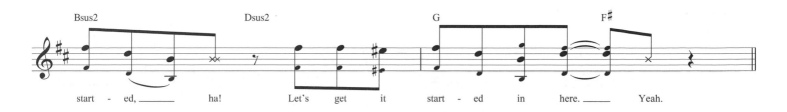

start - ed, _____ ha! Let's get it start - ed in here. _____ Yeah.

Verse

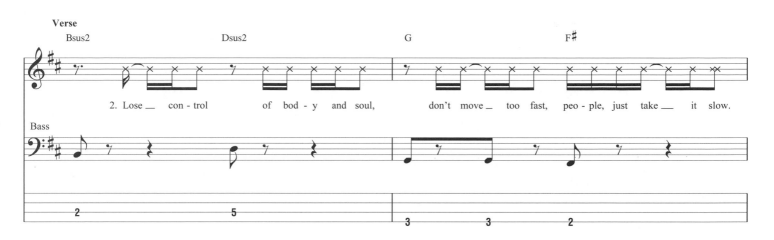

2. Lose _ con - trol of bod - y and soul, don't move _ too fast, peo - ple, just take _ it slow.

Bass

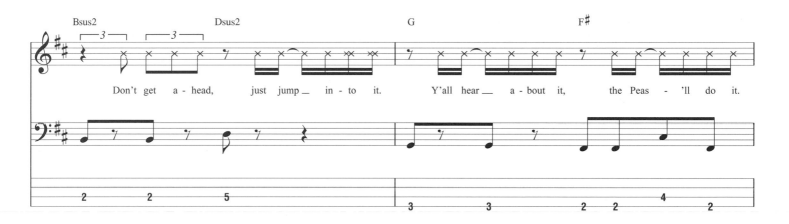

Don't get a - head, just jump _ in - to it. Y'all hear _ a - bout it, the Peas - 'll do it.

Bass: w/ Bass Fig. 2 (3 times)

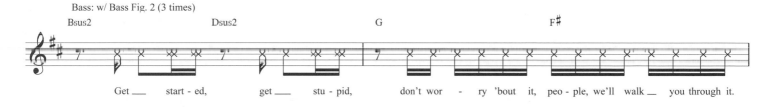

Get _ start - ed, get _ stu - pid, don't wor - ry 'bout it, peo - ple, we'll walk _ you through it.

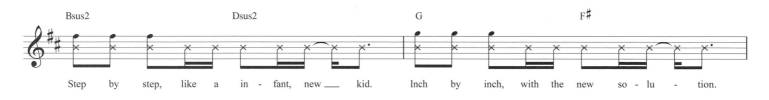

Step by step, like a in - fant, new _ kid. Inch by inch, with the new so - lu - tion.

Trans - mit hits with no de - lu - sion, the feel - ing's ir - re - sist - i - ble and that's how we move _ it.

(The feel - ing's ir - re - sist - i - ble and that's how we move _ it.) _____

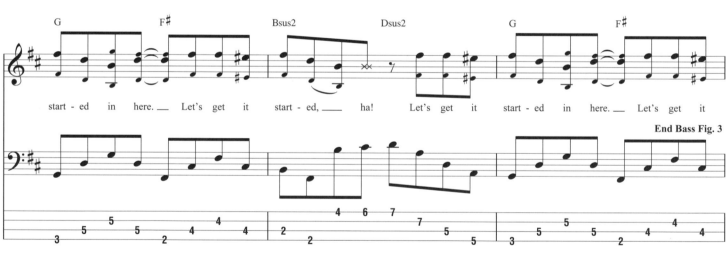

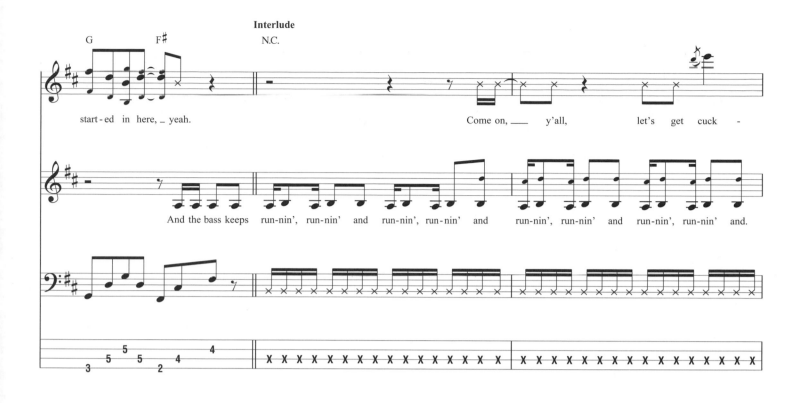

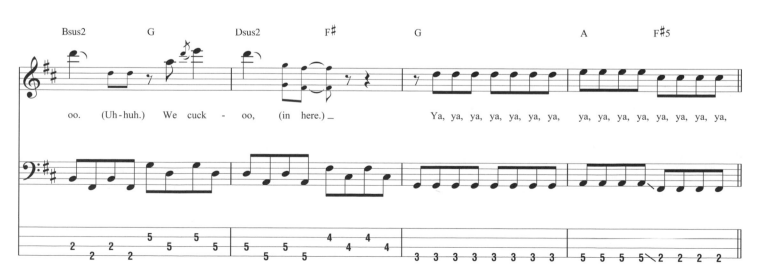

Bridge

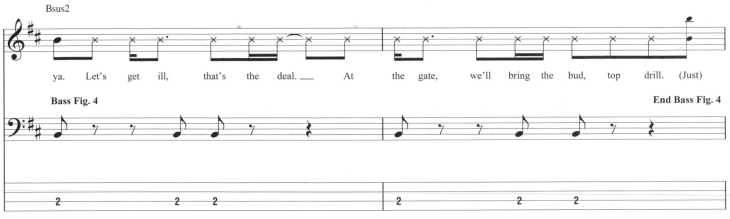

ya. Let's get ill, that's the deal. ___ At the gate, we'll bring the bud, top drill. (Just)

Bass Fig. 4   End Bass Fig. 4

Bass: w/ Bass Fig. 4 (2 times)

lose your mind, this is the time, ___ y'all guessed this ill just to bang your spine. ___ (Just)

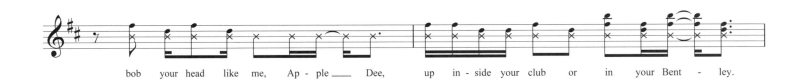

bob your head like me, Ap - ple ___ Dee, up in - side your club or in your Bent - ley.

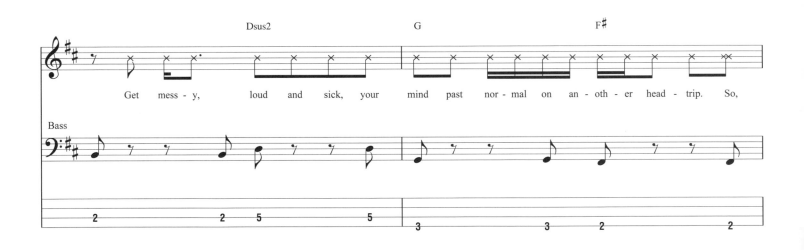

Get mess - y, loud and sick, your mind past nor - mal on an - oth - er head - trip. So,

Bass

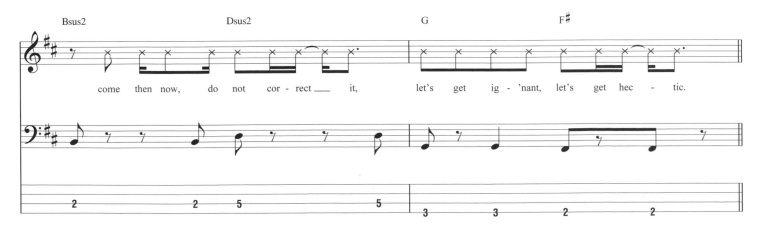

come then now, do not cor - rect ___ it, let's get ig - 'nant, let's get hec - tic.

Pre-Chorus

(Yo!) Ev - 'ry - bod - y, (yeah,) ev - 'ry - bod - y, (yeah,) just get ___ in - to it, (yeah,) and get ___ stu -

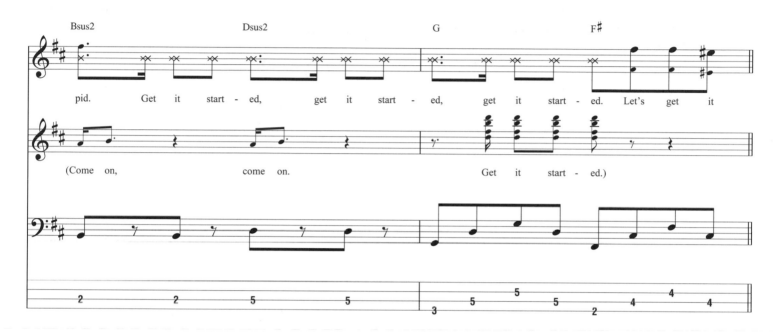

pid. Get it start - ed, get it start - ed, get it start - ed. Let's get it

(Come on, come on. Get it start - ed.)

Chorus
Bass: w/ Bass Fig. 1

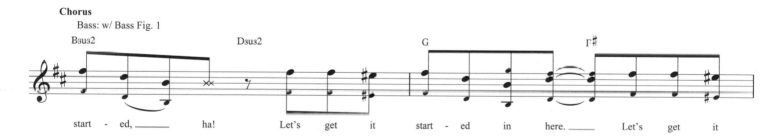

start - ed, ___ ha! Let's get it start - ed in here. ___ Let's get it

Bkgd. Voc.: w/ Voc. Fig. 1   Bass: w/ Bass Fig. 3

start - ed, ___ ha! Let's get it start - ed in here. ___ Let's get it start - ed, ___ ha! Let's get it

Bkgd. Voc.: w/ Voc. Fig. 1

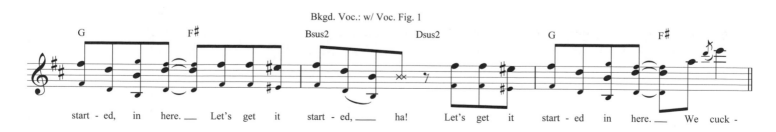

start - ed, in here. ___ Let's get it start - ed, ___ ha! Let's get it start - ed in here. ___ We cuck -

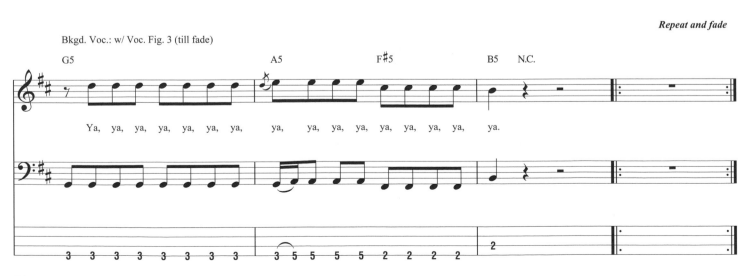

Longview

Words by Billie Joe
Music by Green Day

Tune down 1/2 step:
(low to high) Eb-Ab-Db-Gb

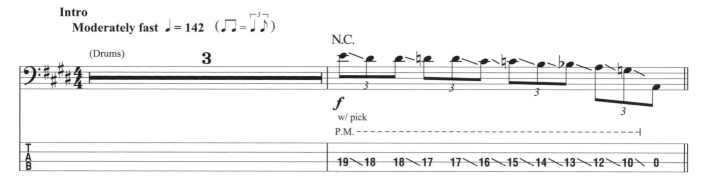

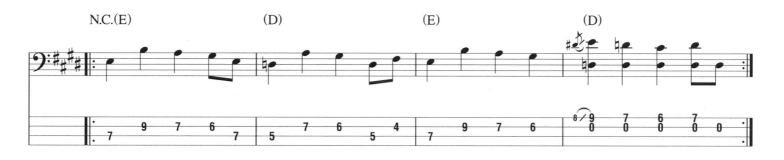

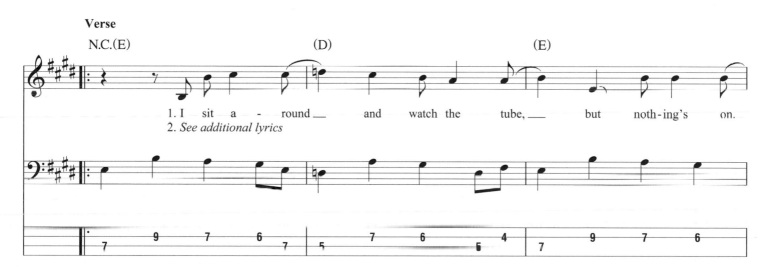

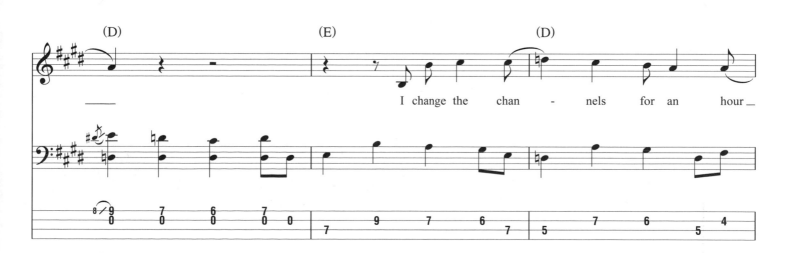

1. I sit a-round _ and watch the tube, _ but noth-ing's on.
2. *See additional lyrics*

I change the chan - nels for an hour _

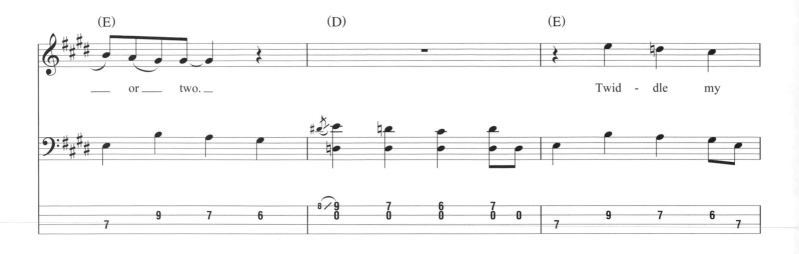

or two. Twid-dle my

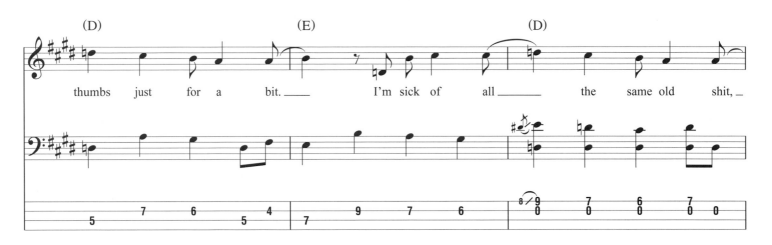

thumbs just for a bit. I'm sick of all the same old shit,

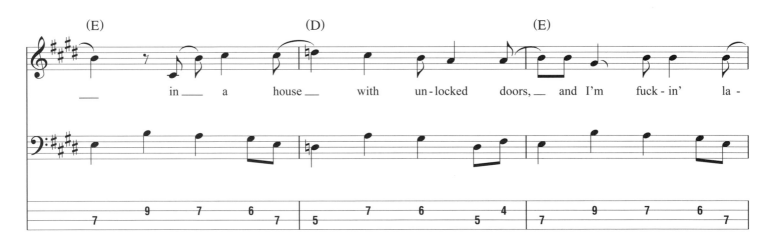

in a house with un-locked doors, and I'm fuck-in' la-

Chorus
Slightly faster ♩ = 150

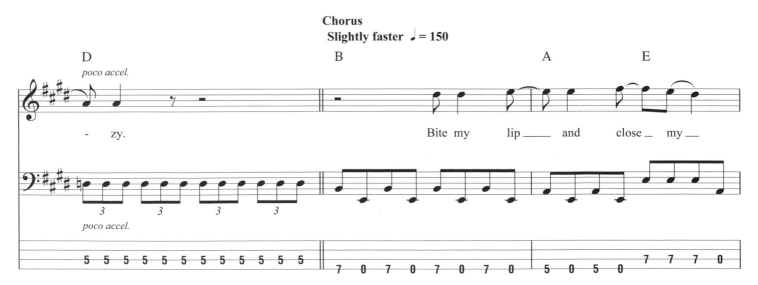

-zy. Bite my lip and close my

Interlude

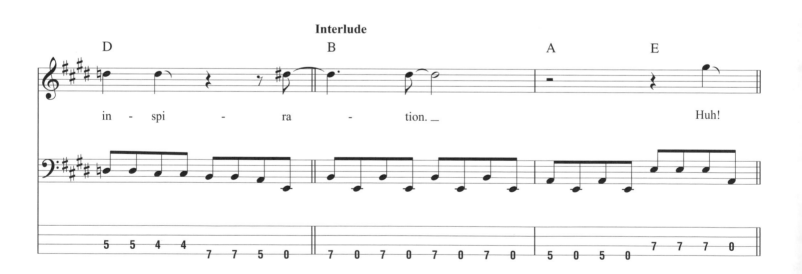

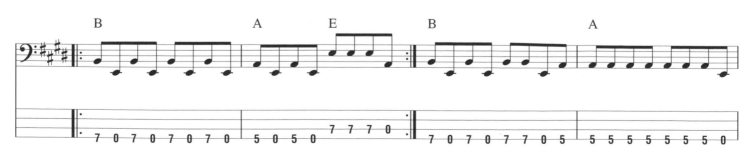

Tempo I

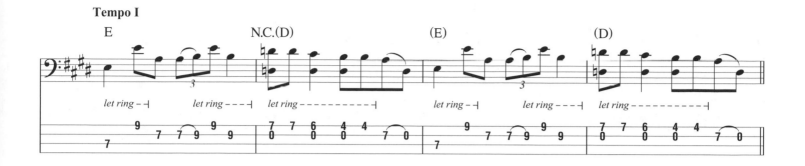

Verse

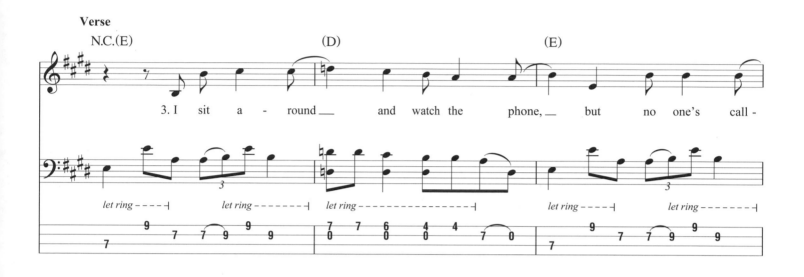

3. I sit a - round ___ and watch the phone, ___ but no one's call -

- ing. Call me pa - thet - ic, call me what ___

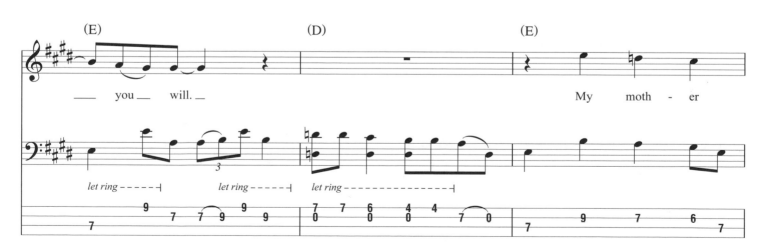

___ you ___ will. ___ My moth - er

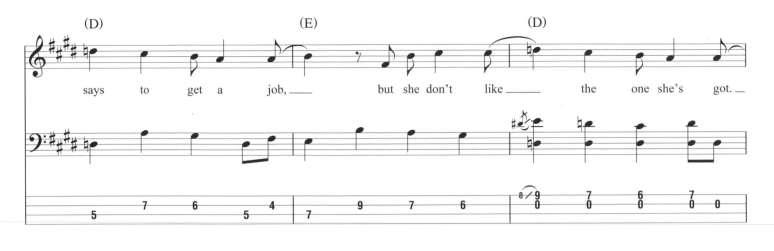

says to get a job, ___ but she don't like ___ the one she's got. ___

___ When mas - tur - ba - tion's lost its fun, ___ you're fuck - in' lone -

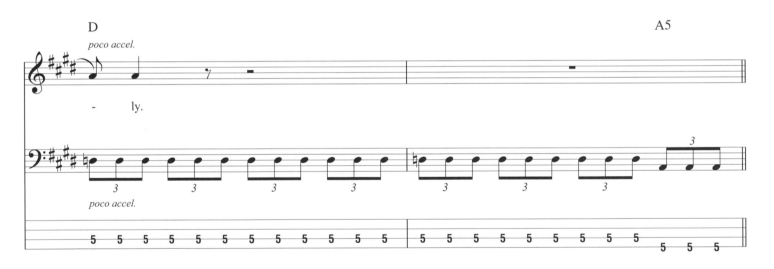

poco accel.

- ly.

poco accel.

Chorus
Tempo II

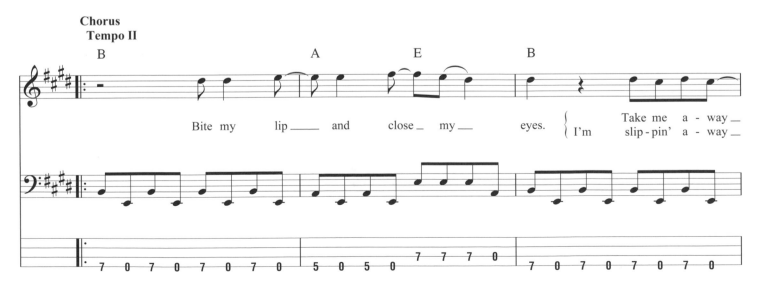

Bite my lip ___ and close ___ my ___ eyes. { Take me a - way
{ I'm slip - pin' a - way ___

Additional Lyrics

2. Peel me off this Velcro seat and get me movin'.
   I sure as hell can't do it by myself.
   I'm feelin' like a dog in heat, barred indoors from the summer street.
   I locked the door to my own cell and I lost the key.

from Creed - *My Own Prison*

My Own Prison

Words and Music by Mark Tremonti and Scott Stapp

Drop D tuning:
(low to high) D-A-D-G

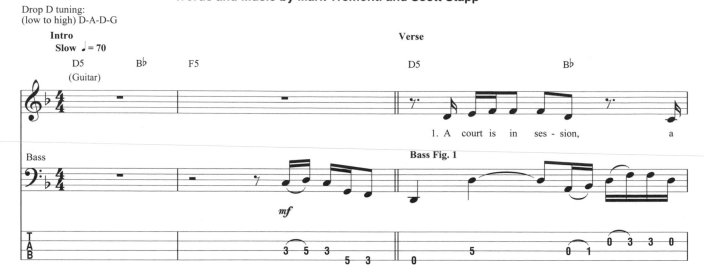

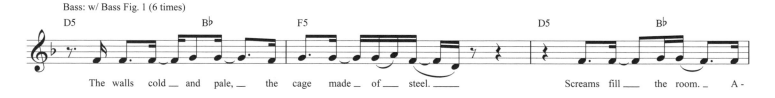

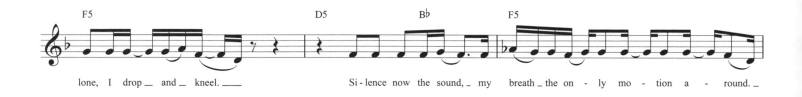

we the meek ___ are all _____ in one. ___

End Voc. Fig. 2

Interlude

2. I hear a thun-der in ___ the dis - tance, ___ see a vi - sion of ___ a cross. ___

Verse

___ I feel the pain that was giv-en on that sad ___ day ___ of ___ loss. _____

Chorus

Bkgd. Voc.: w/ Voc. Fig. 1

Bkgd. Voc.: w/ Voc. Fig. 2

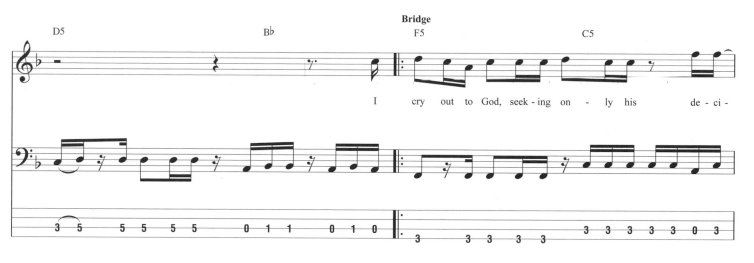

Bkgd. Voc.: w/ Voc. Fig. 1 (2 1/2 times)

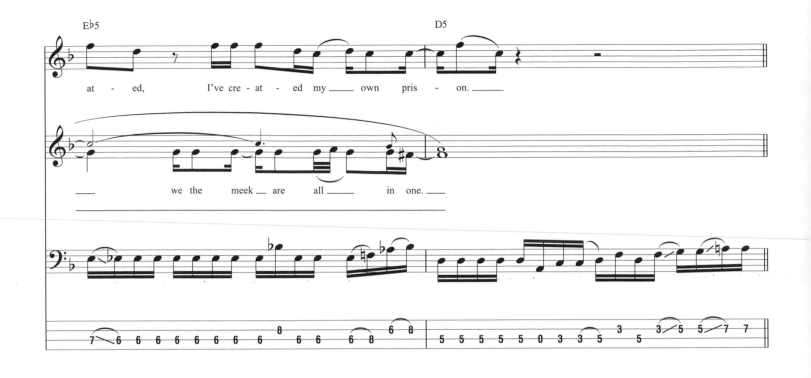

at - ed, I've cre - at - ed my ___ own pris - on. ___

___ we the meek ___ are all ___ in one. ___

Outro-Chorus

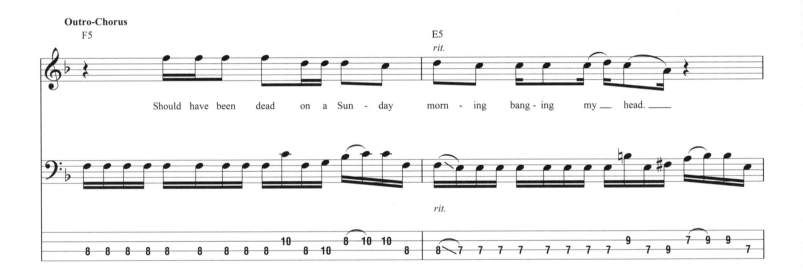

Should have been dead on a Sun - day morn - ing bang - ing my ___ head. ___

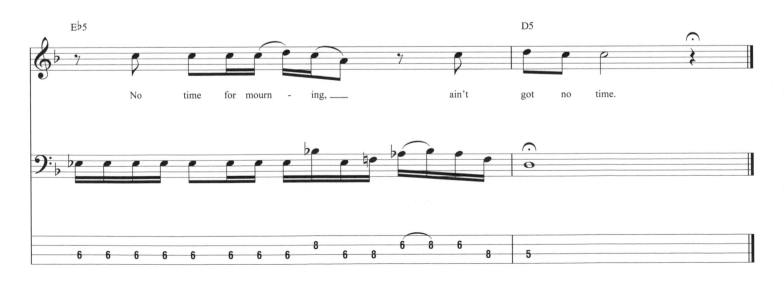

No time for mourn - ing, ___ ain't got no time.

No One Knows

Words and Music by Mark Lanegan, Josh Homme and Nick Oliveri

Tune down 2 steps:
(low to high) C-F-Bb-Eb

Intro
Fast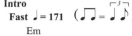

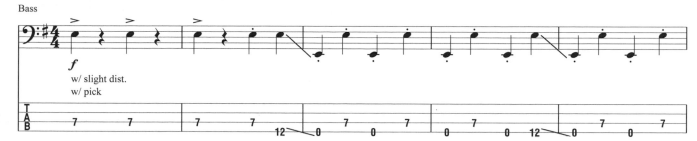

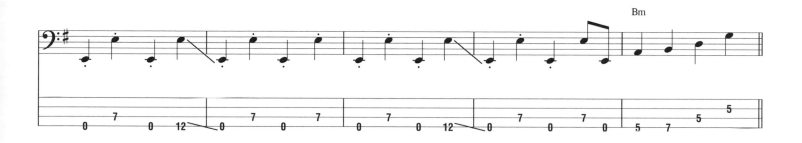

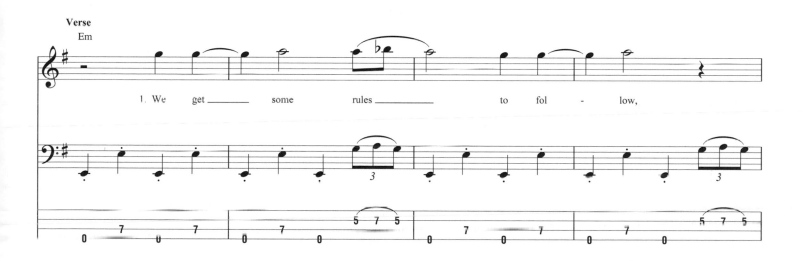

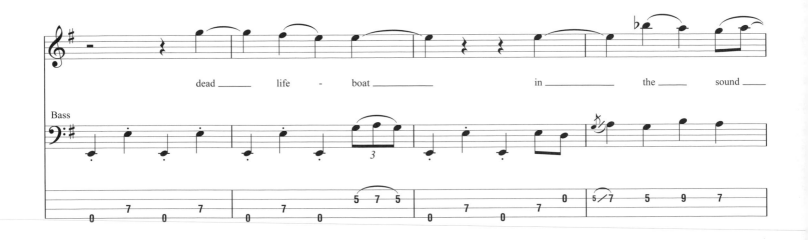

dead _____ life - boat _____ in _____ the _____ sound _____

and come _____ un - done. ___

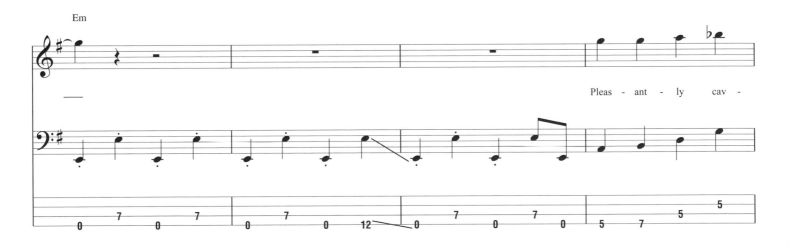

Pleas - ant - ly cav -

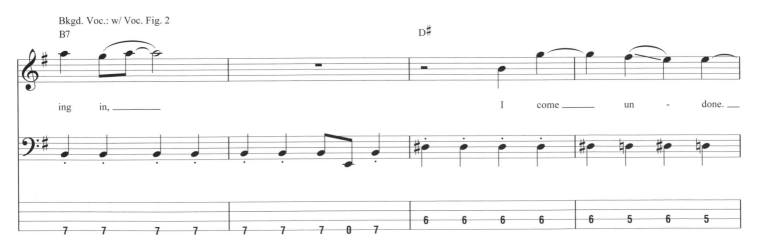

ing in, _____ I come _____ un - done. ___

*Sung 1st time only.

Interlude
E5

Verse
N.C.(E5)   Em7

3. Heav - en _____ smiles _____ a - bove _____ me.

Em

What   a _____ gift _____   there _____ be - low, _____

Bkgd. Voc.: w/ Voc. Fig. 2
B7   D#

_____   but   no _____ one   knows. _____

Outro

Orange Crush

Words and Music by William Berry, Peter Buck, Michael Mills and Michael Stipe

*Lead vocal sings higher pitch 2nd and 3rd times.

*Lead vocal on chorus sung 2nd and 3rd times only.

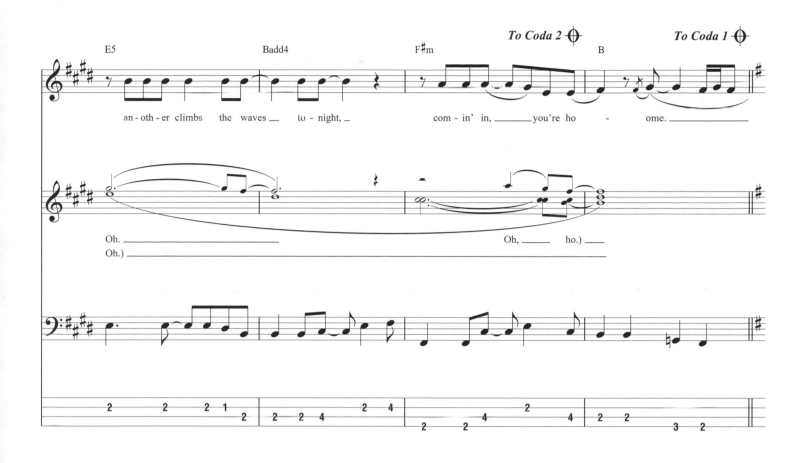

an-oth-er climbs the waves ___ to-night, ___   com-in' in, ___ you're ho - ome. ___

Oh. ___

Oh, ___   ho.) ___

Oh.) ___

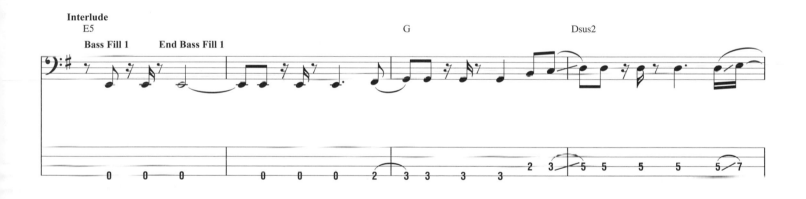

Interlude

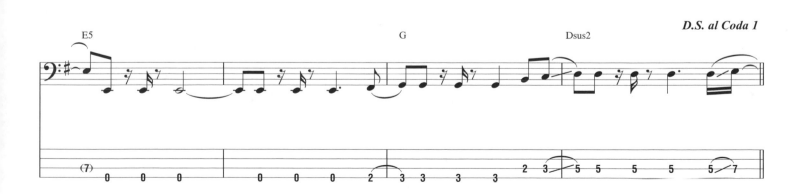

⊕ Coda 1

Breakdown

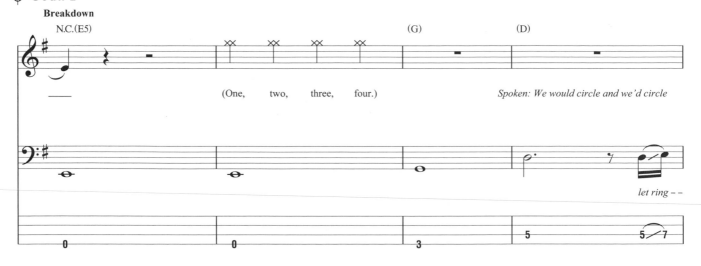

(One, two, three, four.)

Spoken: We would circle and we'd circle

let ring – –

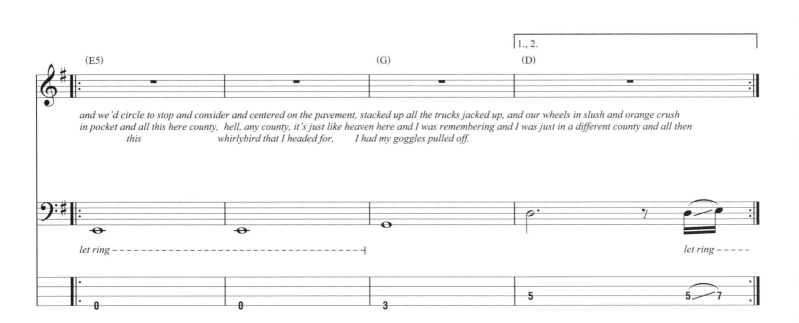

1., 2.

and we'd circle to stop and consider and centered on the pavement, stacked up all the trucks jacked up, and our wheels in slush and orange crush
in pocket and all this here county, hell, any county, it's just like heaven here and I was remembering and I was just in a different county and all then
this   whirlybird that I headed for,   I had my goggles pulled off.

let ring -

let ring - - - - -

3.

D.S. al Coda 2

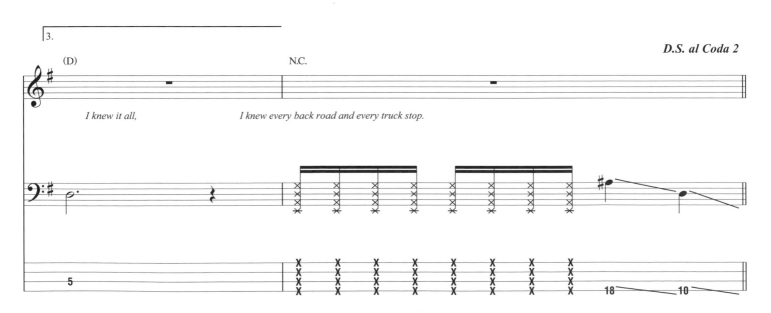

I knew it all,   I knew every back road and every truck stop.

⊕ Coda 2

ome. ___ High ___ on the roof, ___

(Oh. _____
(Oh. _____

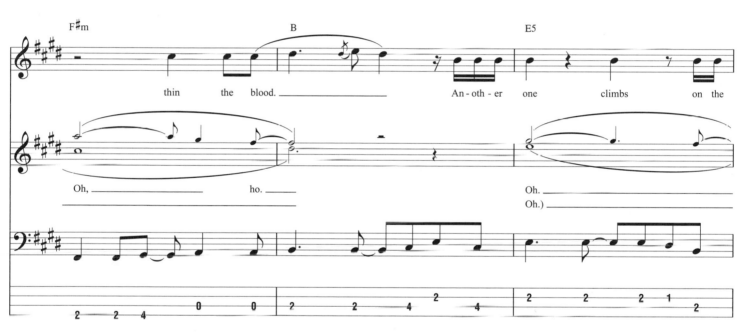

thin the blood. _____ An-oth-er one climbs on the

Oh, _____ ho. _____ Oh. _____
Oh.) _____

waves to-night, __ com-in' in, you're ho - ome. ___

Oh, _____ ho.) ___

from Magic! - *Don't Kill the Magic*

Rude

Words and Music by Nasri Atweh, Mark Pellizzer, Alex Tanas, Ben Spivak and Adam Messinger

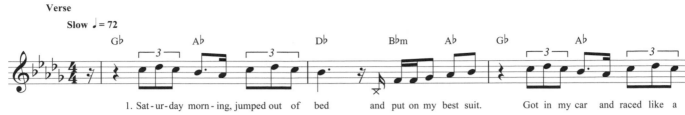

End Bass Fig. 3

And we'll be a fam - i - ly.   Why you got - ta be so

Mar - ry that girl.

rude? _____

Verse

2. I hate to do _____ this, you leave no _____ choice;   can't live with - out her.

Love me or hate me, we will be both   stand - ing at that al - tar,

Bass: w/ Bass Fig. 1

or we will run a - way   to an - oth - er gal - ax - y, _____ you know.

You know she's in love with me, she will go an-y-where I go.
(Mm, where I go.)

Pre-Chorus
Bass: w/ Bass Fig. 2

Can I have your daugh-ter for the rest of my life? ___ Say yes, say yes, 'cause I need to know. You say I'll

nev-er get your bless-ing 'til the day ___ I die, ___ "Tough luck, my friend, 'cause the an-swer's still no."

Chorus
Bass: w/ Bass Fig. 3

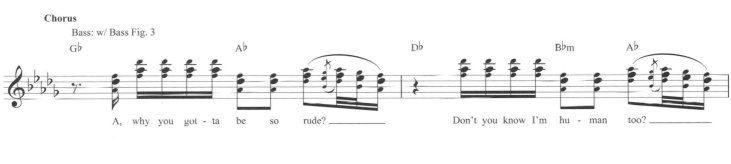

A, why you got-ta be so rude? ___ Don't you know I'm hu-man too? ___

A, why you got-ta be so rude? ___ I'm gon-na mar-ry her an-y-way.

Mar-ry that girl, mar-ry her an-y-way. Mar-ry that girl, no mat-ter what you say.

Mar-ry that girl, we'll be a fam-i-ly. Why you got-ta be so

Bass: w/ Bass Fig. 1

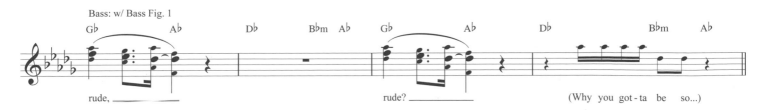

rude, ___ rude? ___ (Why you got-ta be so...)

Guitar Solo

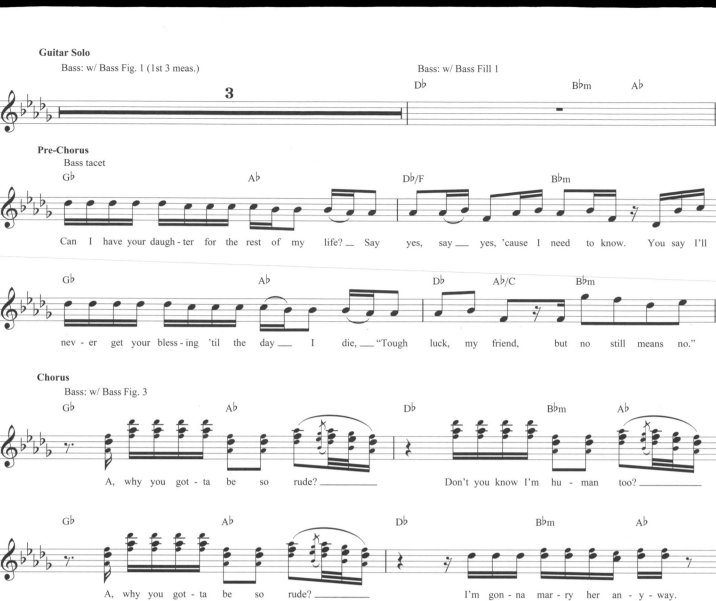

Pre-Chorus

Can I have your daugh-ter for the rest of my life? __ Say yes, say __ yes, 'cause I need to know. You say I'll

nev-er get your bless-ing 'til the day __ I die, __ "Tough luck, my friend, but no still means no."

Chorus

A, why you got-ta be so rude? _____ Don't you know I'm hu-man too? _____

A, why you got-ta be so rude? _____ I'm gon-na mar-ry her an-y-way.

Mar-ry that girl, mar-ry her an-y-way. Mar-ry that girl, no mat-ter what you say.

And we'll be a fam-i-ly.   Why you got-ta be so   rude? _____ Yeah, _
Mar-ry that girl.

ho. Why you got-ta be so   rude? _____   Weh heh. Why you got-ta be so rude? __

Bass Fill 1

Bass

P.M. - - - - - -

from Tool - *Lateralus*

Schism

Words and Music by Maynard James Keenan, Adam Jones, Daniel Carey and Justin Chancellor

Drop D tuning:
(low to high) D-A-D-G

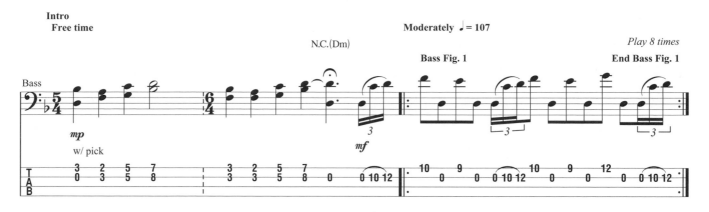

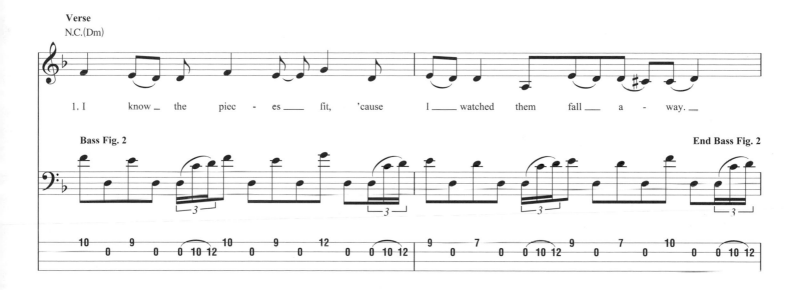

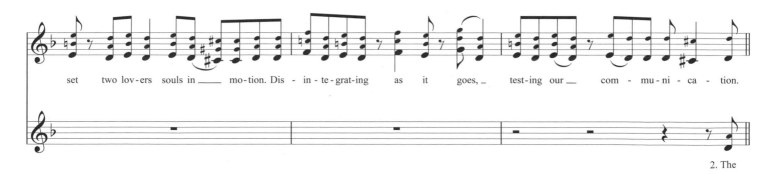

2. The

Verse

Bass: w/ Bass Fig. 1 (2 times)

light that fueled __ our fire __ then __ has burned _ a hole __ be - tween us, so __ we

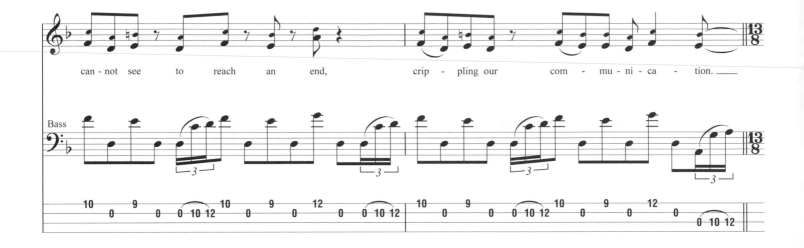

can - not see to reach an end, crip - pling our com - mu - ni - ca - tion.

Interlude

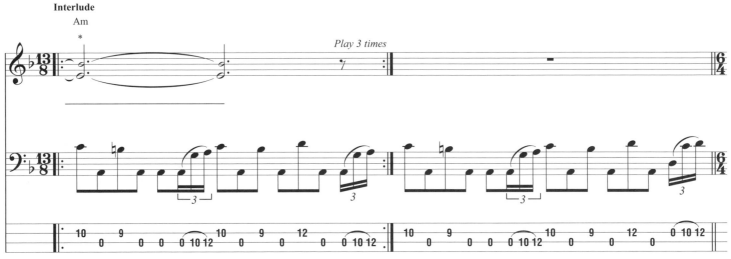

*Sung 1st time only.

 Verse

Bass: w/ Bass Fig. 2 (3 times)

Dm

3. I know __ the piec - es __ fit, 'cause I __ watched them tum - ble __ down. __
was a time that the piec - es __ fit, but I __ watched them fall __ a - way. __

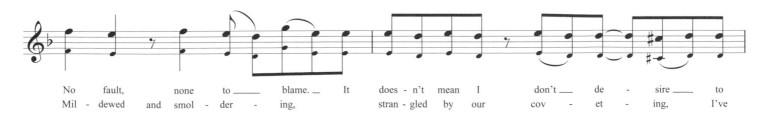

No fault, none to __ blame. __ It does - n't mean I don't __ de - sire __ to
Mil - dewed and smol - der - ing, stran - gled by our cov - et - ing, I've

point the fin - ger, blame __ the __ oth - er. Watch the tem - ple top - ple __ o - ver. To
done the math e - nough to __ know __ the dan - gers of our sec - ond gues - sing.

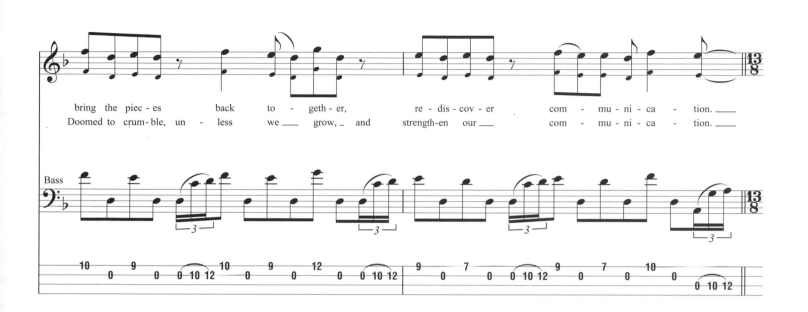

bring the piec - es back to - geth - er, re - dis - cov - er com - mu - ni - ca - tion. __
Doomed to crum - ble, un - less we __ grow, __ and strength-en our __ com - mu - ni - ca - tion. __

Bass

Interlude

Am

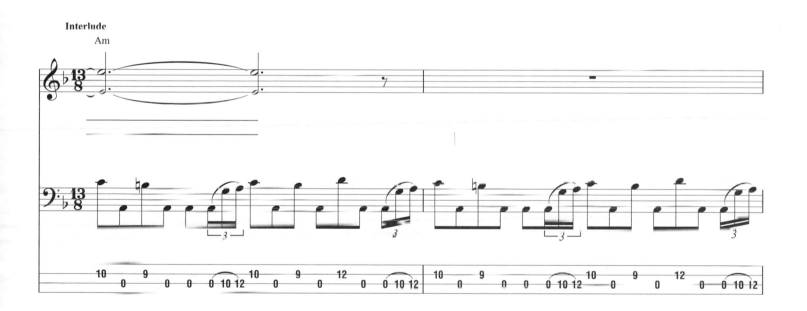

To Coda ⊕

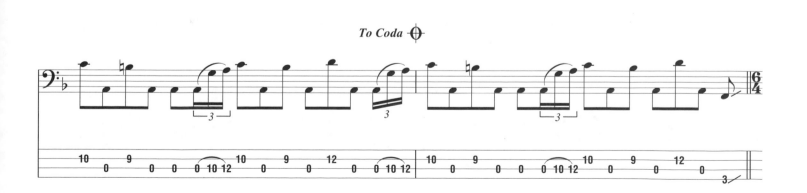

Bridge

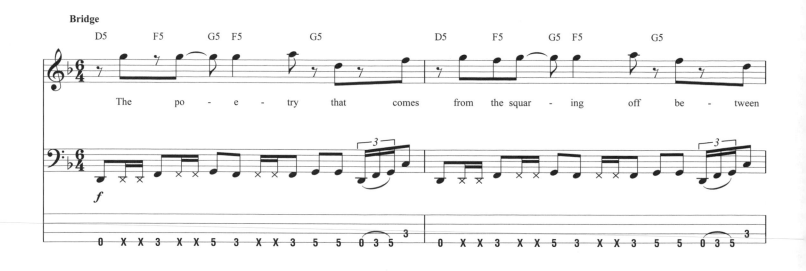

The po - e - try that comes from the squar - ing off be - tween

and the cir - cl - ing is worth it. Find - ing beau - ty in the dis - so - nance.

D.S. al Coda $\oplus$ **Coda**

N.C.(Dm)

4. There

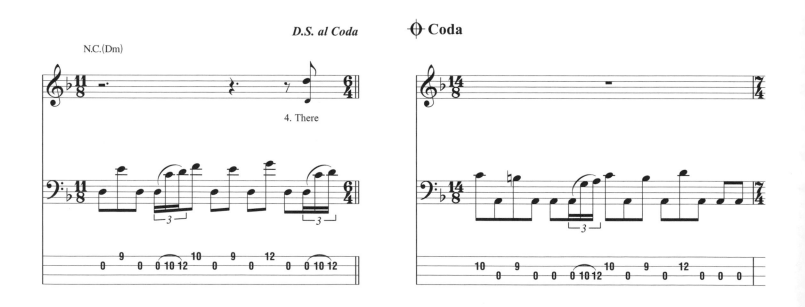

let ring – – let ring   *let ring – – let ring*   *let ring – – let ring*

Interlude

Am

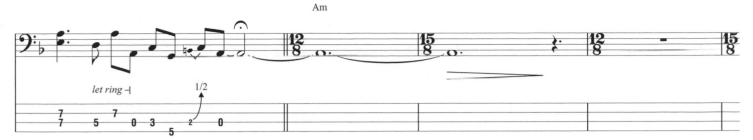

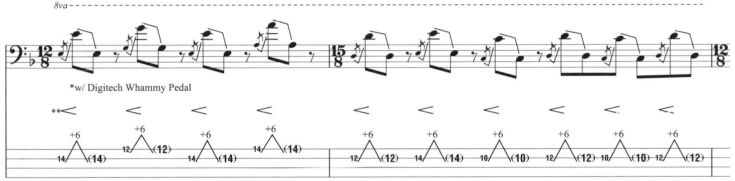

*w/ Digitech Whammy Pedal

*Set for one octave above.
**Vol. swell, next 8 meas.

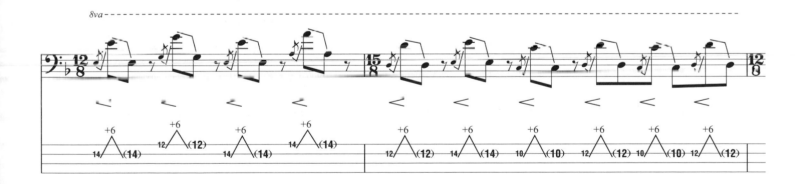

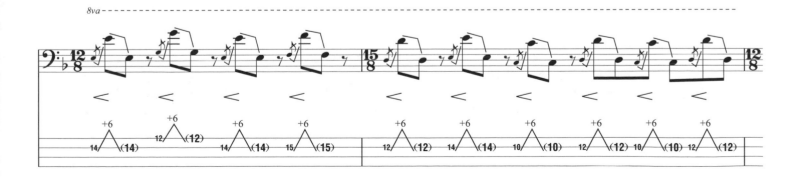

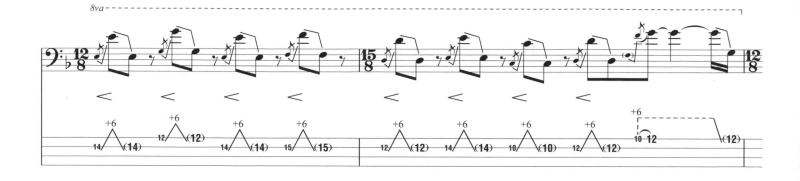

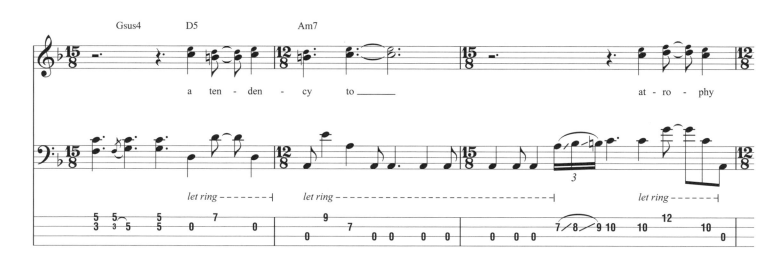

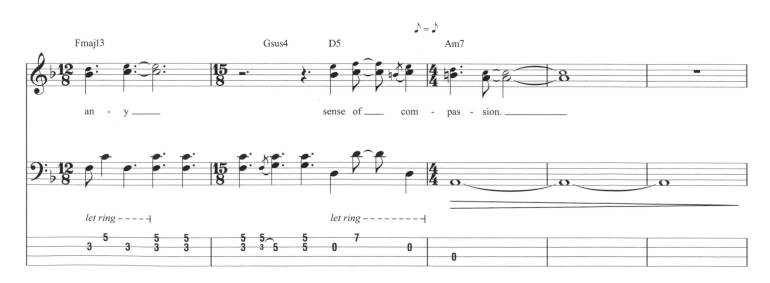

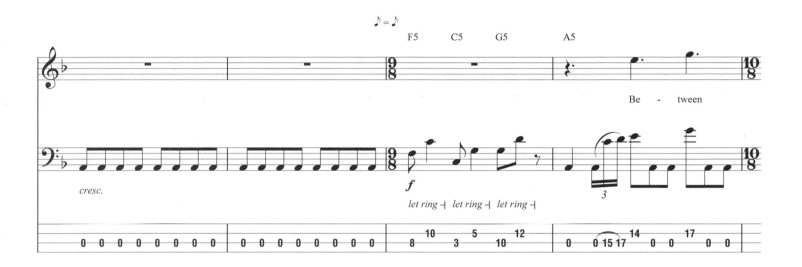

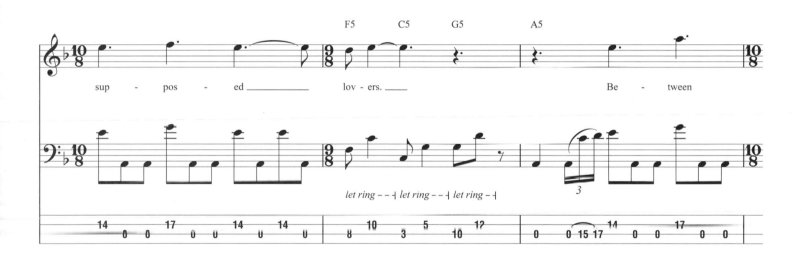

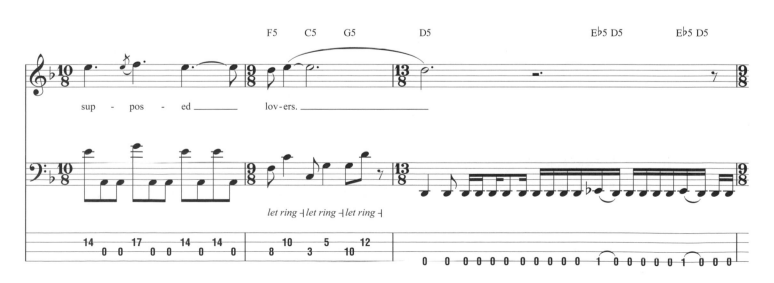

116

from The White Stripes - *Elephant*

Seven Nation Army

Words and Music by Jack White

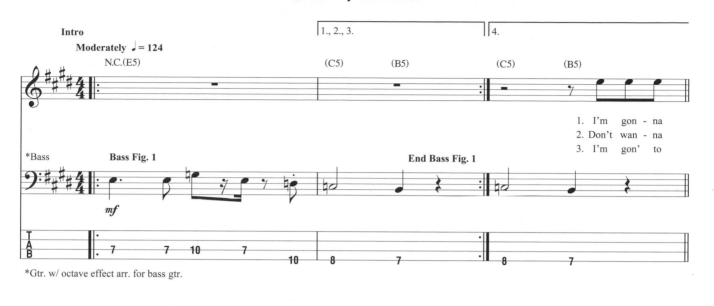

*Gtr. w/ octave effect arr. for bass gtr.

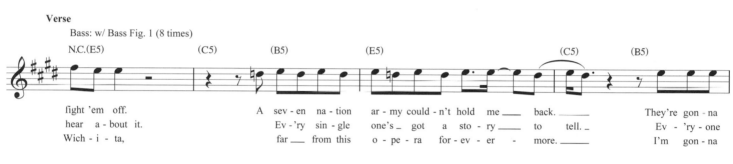

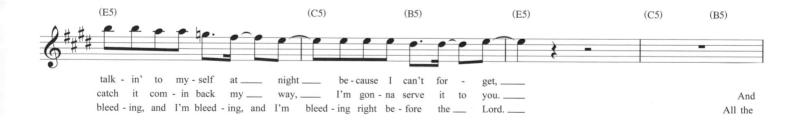

mes - sage com - in' from my eyes says leave it a - lone.
feel - ing com - in' from my bones says find a home.
stains com - in' from my blood tell me, "Go back home."

Coda 1

Guitar Solo

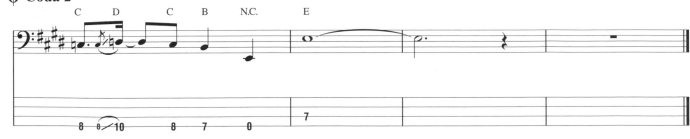

Coda 2

from Bruno Mars - *Unorthodox Jukebox*

Treasure

Words and Music by Bruno Mars, Ari Levine, Philip Lawrence, Fredrick Brown and Thibaut Berland

from Mark Ronson - *Uptown Special*

Uptown Funk

Words and Music by Mark Ronson, Bruno Mars, Philip Lawrence, Jeff Bhasker, Devon Gallaspy, Nicholaus Williams, Lonnie Simmons, Ronnie Wilson, Charles Wilson, Rudolph Taylor and Robert Wilson

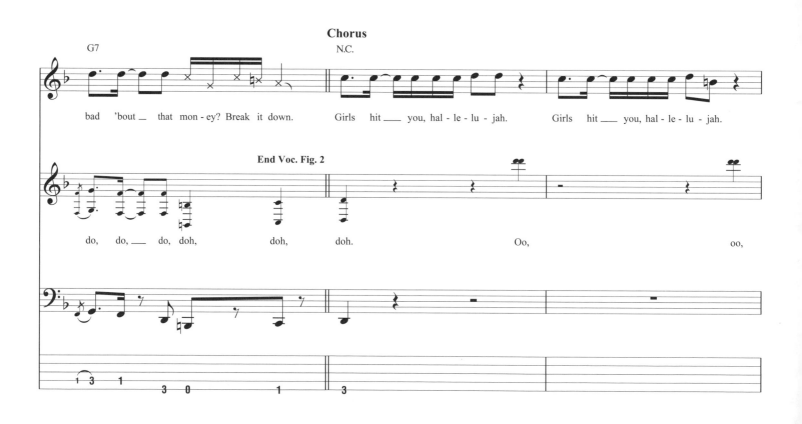

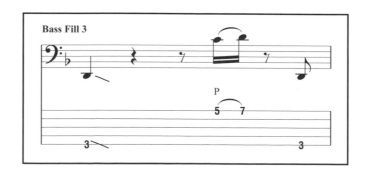

Girls hit ___ you, hal - le - lu - jah. 'Cause up - town funk gon' give it to ya. 'Cause

oo, oo.)

('Cause up - town funk gon' give it to ya.

up - town funk gon' give it to ya. Sat - ur - day night ___ and we in the spot. ___ Don't be - lieve ___ me? Just watch. Come on!

Sat - ur - day night ___ and we in the spot.) ___

§ Interlude

Dm7   G7   Dm7   G7

Don't be - lieve ___ me? Just watch, uh!

(Ha!)

Voc Fig. 3   **End Voc Fig. 3**

(Doh,   doh, do, do, doh, do do, doh, doh.   Doh, do, do, doh, do.)

125

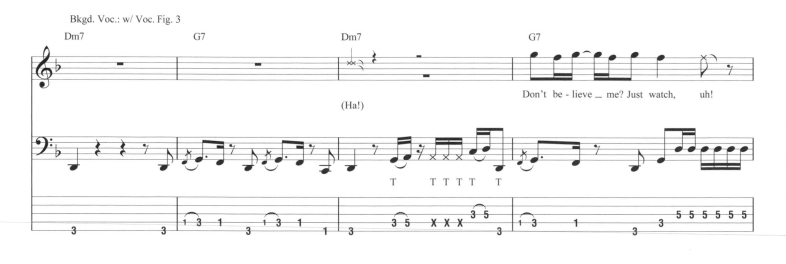

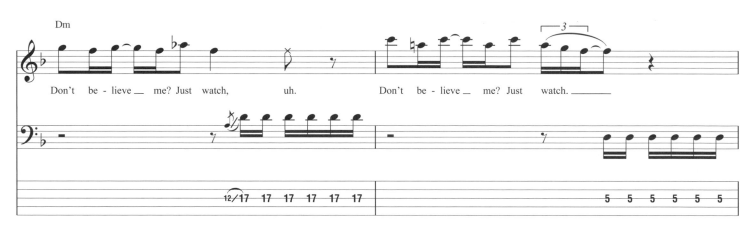

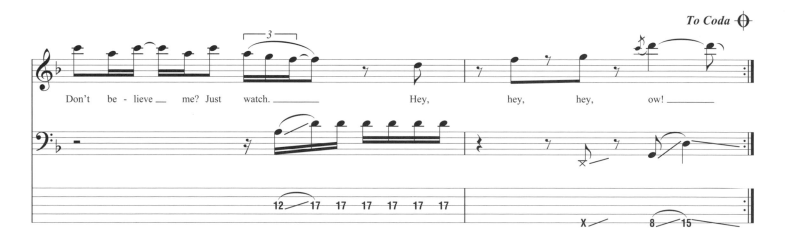

Bridge

Bass: w/ Bass Fig. 1 (4 times)
Bkgd. Voc.: w/ Voc. Fig. 1

Bkgd. Voc.: w/ Voc. Fig. 2

from Kings of Leon - *Only by the Night*

Use Somebody

Words and Music by Caleb Followill, Nathan Followill, Jared Followill and Matthew Followill

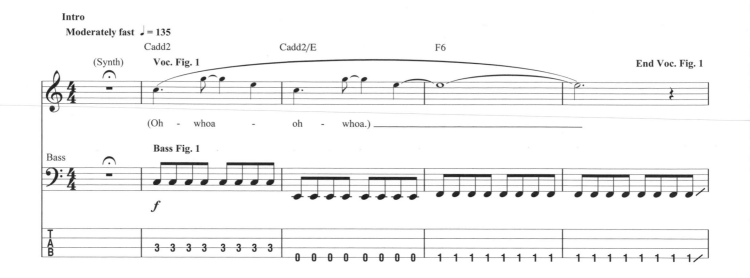

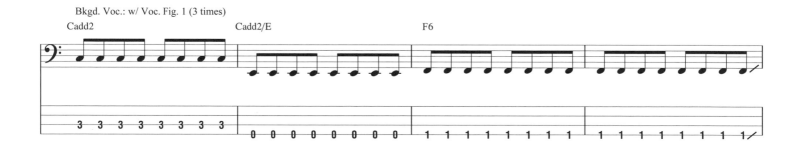

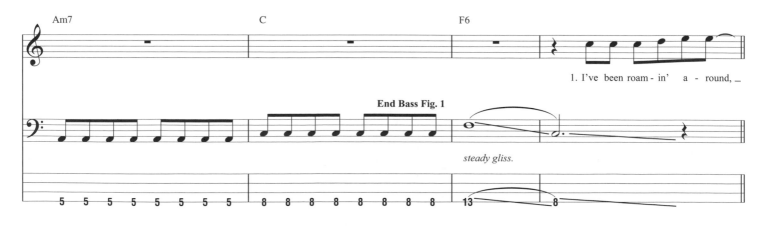

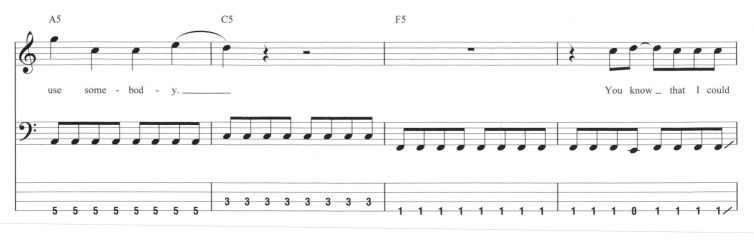

use some-bod - y. _____ You know _ that I could

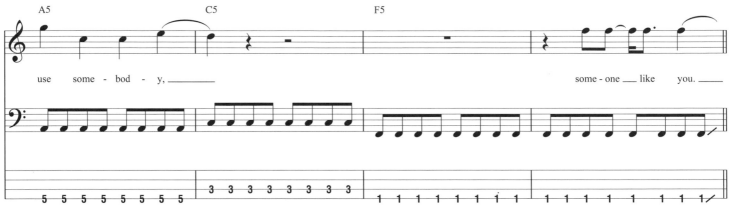

use some-bod - y, _____ some - one _ like you. _____

Chorus
Bkgd. Voc.: w/ Voc. Fig. 1 (4 times)
Bass: w/ Bass Fig. 1

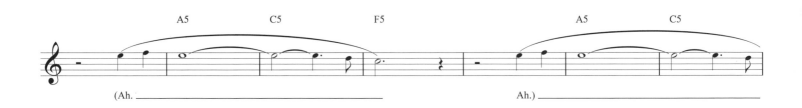

(Ah. _____ Ah.) _____

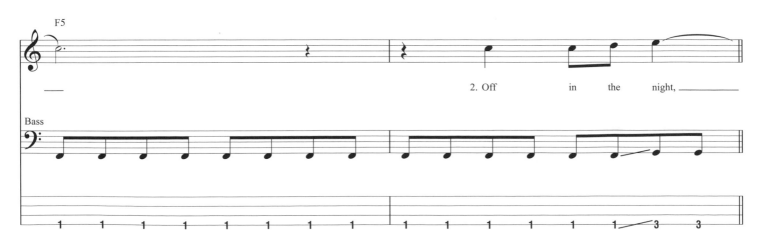

_____ 2. Off in the night, _____

Bass

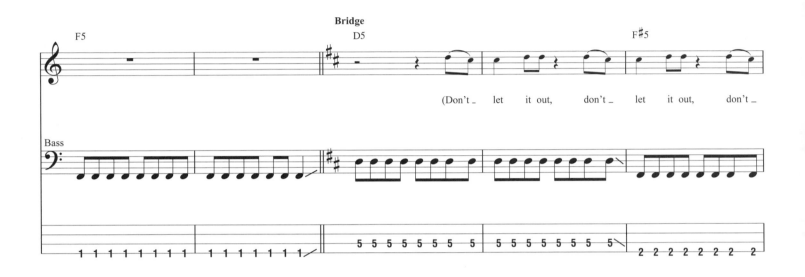

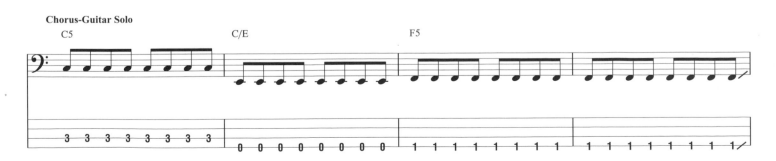

BASS NOTATION LEGEND

Bass music can be notated two different ways: on a *musical staff*, and in *tablature*.

THE MUSICAL STAFF shows pitches and rhythms and is divided by bar lines into measures. Pitches are named after the first seven letters of the alphabet.

TABLATURE graphically represents the bass fingerboard. Each horizontal line represents a string, and each number represents a fret.

Notes:

Strings:
high
low

3rd string, open   2nd string, 2nd fret   1st & 2nd strings open, played together

HAMMER-ON: Strike the first (lower) note with one finger, then sound the higher note (on the same string) with another finger by fretting it without picking.

PULL-OFF: Place both fingers on the notes to be sounded. Strike the first note and without picking, pull the finger off to sound the second (lower) note.

LEGATO SLIDE: Strike the first note and then slide the same fret-hand finger up or down to the second note. The second note is not struck.

SHIFT SLIDE: Same as legato slide, except the second note is struck.

TRILL: Very rapidly alternate between the notes indicated by continuously hammering on and pulling off.

TREMOLO PICKING: The note is picked as rapidly and continuously as possible.

VIBRATO: The string is vibrated by rapidly bending and releasing the note with the fretting hand.

SHAKE: Using one finger, rapidly alternate between two notes on one string by sliding either a half-step above or below.

NATURAL HARMONIC: Strike the note while the fret hand lightly touches the string directly over the fret indicated.

MUFFLED STRINGS: A percussive sound is produced by laying the fret hand across the string(s) without depressing them and striking them with the pick hand.

BEND: Strike the note and bend up the interval shown.

BEND AND RELEASE: Strike the note and bend up as indicated, then release back to the original note. Only the first note is struck.

RIGHT-HAND TAP: Hammer ("tap") the fret indicated with the "pick-hand" index or middle finger and pull off to the note fretted by the fret hand.

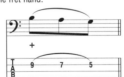

LEFT-HAND TAP: Hammer ("tap") the fret indicated with the "fret-hand" index or middle finger.

SLAP: Strike ("slap") string with right-hand thumb.

POP: Snap ("pop") string with right-hand index or middle finger.

Additional Musical Definitions

(accent) • Accentuate note (play it louder).

(accent) • Accentuate note with great intensity.

(staccato) • Play the note short.

• Downstroke

V

• Upstroke

D.S. al Coda

• Go back to the sign (𝄋), then play until the measure marked "*To Coda*," then skip to the section labelled "**Coda**."

D.C. al Fine

• Go back to the beginning of the song and play until the measure marked "*Fine*" (end).

Bass Fig.

• Label used to recall a recurring pattern.

Fill

• Label used to identify a brief melodic figure which is to be inserted into the arrangement.

tacet

• Instrument is silent (drops out).

• Repeat measures between signs.

• When a repeated section has different endings, play the first ending only the first time and the second ending only the second time.

NOTE: Tablature numbers in parentheses mean:
1. The note is being sustained over a system (note in standard notation is tied), or
2. The note is sustained, but a new articulation (such as a hammer-on, pull-off, slide or vibrato) begins.